PARKINSON'S LAW

PARKINSON'S LAW

AND OTHER STUDIES IN ADMINISTRATION

BY

C. Northcote Parkinson

ILLUSTRATED BY

Robert C. Osborn

HOUGHTON MIFFLIN COMPANY BOSTON

PRINTED IN THE U.S.A.

Thirty-Second Printing   C

for Ann

PREFACE

TO THE VERY YOUNG, to schoolteachers, as also to those who compile textbooks about constitutional history, politics, and current affairs, the world is a more or less rational place. They visualize the election of representatives, freely chosen from among those the people trust. They picture the process by which the wisest and best of these become ministers of state. They imagine how captains of industry, freely elected by shareholders, choose for managerial responsibility those who have proved their ability in a humbler role. Books exist in which assumptions such as these are boldly stated or tacitly implied. To those, on the other hand, with any experience of affairs, these assumptions are merely ludicrous. Solemn conclaves of the wise and good are mere figments of the teacher's mind. It is salutary, therefore, if an occasional warning is uttered on this subject. Heaven forbid that students should cease to read books on the science of public or business administration — provided only that these works are classified as fiction. Placed between the novels of Rider Haggard and H. G. Wells, intermingled with volumes about ape men and space ships, these textbooks could harm no one. Placed elsewhere, among works of reference, they can do more damage than might at first sight seem possible.

Dismayed to realize what other people suppose to be the truth about civil servants or building plans, I have occasionally tried to provide, for those interested, a glimpse of reality. The reader of discrimination will guess that these glimpses of the truth are based on no ordinary experience. In the expectation, moreover, that some readers will have less discrimination than others, I have been careful to hint, occasionally, casually, at the vast amount of research upon which my theories are founded. Let the reader picture to himself the wall charts, card index cabinets, calculating machines, slide rules, and reference works that may be thought the indispensable background to a study such as this. Let him then be assured that the reality dwarfs all his imagining, and that the truths here revealed are the work not merely of an admittedly gifted individual but of a vast and costly research establishment. An occasional reader may feel that more detailed description should have been given of the experiments and calculations upon which these theories rest. Let him reflect, however, that a volume so elaborate would take longer to read and cost more to buy.

While it is undeniable that each one of these essays embodies the results from years of patient investigation, it must not be supposed that all has yet been told. The recent discovery in a certain field of warfare that the number of the enemy killed varies inversely with the number of generals on one's own side has opened a whole new field of research. A new significance has been quite recently attributed to the illegibility of signatures, the attempt being made to fix the point in a successful executive career at which the handwriting becomes meaningless even to the executive himself. New developments occur almost daily, making it virtually certain that later editions of this work will quickly supersede the first.

I wish to thank the editors who have given permission to reprint certain of these essays. Pride of place must go to the editor of *The Economist,* the journal in which Parkinson's law was first revealed to mankind. To the same editor I am indebted for permission to reprint the essay on "Directors and Councils," as also that on "Pension Point." Certain of the other articles have also appeared previously in *Harper's Magazine* and *The Reporter.*

To the artist, Robert C. Osborn, I am deeply grateful for adding a touch of frivolity to a work that might otherwise have seemed too technical for the general reader. To the publishers I am indebted for their encouragement, without which I should have attempted little and achieved still less. Last of all, I place on record the gratitude I feel toward the higher mathematician with whose science the reader is occasionally blinded and to whom (but for other reasons) this book is dedicated.

C. NORTHCOTE PARKINSON

Singapore
1957

CONTENTS

PARKINSON'S LAW

1
PARKINSON'S LAW
OR THE RISING PYRAMID

WORK EXPANDS so as to fill the time available for its completion. General recognition of this fact is shown in the proverbial phrase "It is the busiest man who has time to spare." Thus, an elderly lady of leisure can spend the entire day in writing and dispatching a postcard to her niece at Bognor Regis. An hour will be spent in finding the postcard, another in hunting for spectacles, half an hour in a search for the address, an hour and a quarter in composition, and twenty minutes in deciding whether or not to take an umbrella when going to the mailbox in the next street. The total effort that would occupy a busy man for three minutes all told may in this fashion leave another person prostrate after a day of doubt, anxiety, and toil.

Granted that work (and especially paperwork) is thus elastic in its demands on time, it is manifest that there need be little or no relationship between the work to be done and the size of the staff to which it may be assigned. A lack of real activity does not, of necessity, result in leisure. A lack of occupation is not necessarily revealed by a manifest idleness. The thing to be done swells in importance and complexity in a direct ratio with the time to be spent. This fact is widely recognized, but less attention has been paid to its wider implications, more especially in the field of public administration. Politicians and taxpayers have assumed (with occasional phases of doubt) that a rising total in the number of civil servants must reflect a growing volume of work to be done. Cynics, in questioning this belief, have

imagined that the multiplication of officials must have left some of them idle or all of them able to work for shorter hours. But this is a matter in which faith and doubt seem equally misplaced. The fact is that the number of the officials and the quantity of the work are not related to each other at all. The rise in the total of those employed is governed by Parkinson's Law and would be much the same whether the volume of the work were to increase, diminish, or even disappear. The importance of Parkinson's Law lies in the fact that it is a law of growth based upon an analysis of the factors by which that growth is controlled.

The validity of this recently discovered law must rest mainly on statistical proofs, which will follow. Of more interest to the general reader is the explanation of the factors underlying the general tendency to which this law gives definition. Omitting technicalities (which are numerous) we may distinguish at the outset two motive forces. They can be represented for the present purpose by two almost axiomatic statements, thus: (1) "An official wants to multiply subordinates, not rivals" and (2) "Officials make work for each other."

To comprehend Factor 1, we must picture a civil servant, called A, who finds himself overworked. Whether this overwork is real or imaginary is immaterial, but we should observe, in passing, that A's sensation (or illusion) might easily result from his own decreasing energy: a normal symptom of middle age. For this real or imagined overwork there are, broadly speaking, three possible remedies. He may resign; he may ask to halve the work with a colleague called B; he may demand the assistance of two subordinates, to be called C and D. There is probably no instance

4

in history, however, of A choosing any but the third alternative. By resignation he would lose his pension rights. By having B appointed, on his own level in the hierarchy, he would merely bring in a rival for promotion to W's vacancy when W (at long last) retires. So A would rather have C and D, junior men, below him. They will add to his consequence and, by dividing the work into two categories, as between C and D, he will have the merit of being the only man who comprehends them both. It is essential to realize at this point that C and D are, as it were, inseparable. To appoint C alone would have been impossible. Why? Because C, if by himself, would divide the work with A and so assume almost the equal status that has been refused in the first instance to B; a status the more emphasized if C is A's only possible successor. Subordinates must thus number two or more, each being thus kept in order by fear of the other's promotion. When C complains in turn of being overworked (as he certainly will) A will, with the concurrence of C, advise the appointment of two assistants to help C. But he can then avert internal friction only by advising the appointment of two more assistants to help D, whose position is much the same. With this recruitment of E, F, G, and H the promotion of A is now practically certain.

Seven officials are now doing what one did before. This is where Factor 2 comes into operation. For these seven make so much work for each other that all are fully occupied and A is actually working harder than ever. An incoming document may well come before each of them in turn. Official E decides that it falls within the province of F, who places a draft reply before C, who amends it drastically before consulting D, who asks G to deal with it. But G goes on leave at this point, handing the file over to H, who drafts a minute that is signed by D and returned to C, who revises his draft accordingly and lays the new version before A.

What does A do? He would have every excuse for signing the thing unread, for he has many other matters on his mind. Knowing now that he is to succeed W next year, he has to decide whether C or D should succeed to his own office. He had to agree to G's going on leave even if not yet strictly entitled to it. He is worried whether H should not have gone instead, for reasons of health. He has looked pale recently — partly but not solely because of his domestic troubles. Then there is the business of F's special increment of salary for the period of the conference and E's application for transfer to the Ministry of Pensions. A has heard that D is in love with a married typist and that G and F are no longer on speaking terms — no one seems to know why. So A might be tempted to sign C's draft and have done with it. But A is a conscientious man. Beset as he is with problems created by his colleagues for themselves and for him — created by the mere fact of these officials' existence — he is not the man to shirk his duty. He reads through the draft with care, deletes the fussy paragraphs added by C and H, and restores the thing back to the form preferred in the first instance by the able (if quarrelsome) F. He corrects the English — none of these young men can write grammatically — and finally produces the same reply he would have written if officials C to H had never been born. Far more people have taken far longer to produce the same result. No one has been idle. All have done their best. And it is late in the evening before A finally quits his office and begins the return journey to Ealing. The last of

6

the office lights are being turned off in the gathering dusk that marks the end of another day's administrative toil. Among the last to leave, A reflects with bowed shoulders and a wry smile that late hours, like gray hairs, are among the penalties of success.

From this description of the factors at work the student of political science will recognize that administrators are more or less bound to multiply. Nothing has yet been said, however, about the period of time likely to elapse between the date of A's appointment and the date from which we can calculate the pensionable service of H. Vast masses of statistical evidence have been collected and it is from a study of this data that Parkinson's Law has been deduced. Space will not allow of detailed analysis but the reader will be interested to know that research began in the British Navy Estimates. These were chosen because the Admiralty's responsibilities are more easily measurable than those of, say, the Board of Trade. The question is merely one of numbers and tonnage. Here are some typical figures. The strength of the Navy in 1914 could be shown as 146,000 officers and men, 3249 dockyard officials and clerks, and 57,000 dockyard workmen. By 1928 there were only 100,000 officers and men and only 62,439 workmen, but the dockyard officials and clerks by then numbered 4558. As for warships, the strength in 1928 was a mere fraction of what it had been in 1914 — fewer than 20 capital ships in commission as compared with 62. Over the same period the Admiralty officials had increased in number from 2000 to 3569, providing (as was remarked) "a magnificent navy on land." These figures are more clearly set forth in tabular form.

ADMIRALTY STATISTICS

Year	Capital ships in commission	Officers and men in R.N.	Dockyard workers	Dockyard officials and clerks	Admiralty officials
1914	62	146,000	57,000	3249	2000
1928	20	100,000	62,439	4558	3569
Increase or Decrease	−67.74%	−31.5%	+9.54%	+40.28%	+78.45%

The criticism voiced at the time centered on the ratio between the numbers of those available for fighting and those available only for administration. But that comparison is not to the present purpose. What we have to note is that the 2000 officials of 1914 had become the 3569 of 1928; and that this growth was unrelated to any possible increase in their work. The Navy during that period had diminished, in point of fact, by a third in men and two-thirds in ships. Nor, from 1922 onward, was its strength even expected to increase; for its total of ships (unlike its total of officials) was limited by the Washington Naval Agreement of that year. Here we have then a 78 per cent increase over a period of fourteen years; an average of 5.6 per cent increase a year on the earlier total. In fact, as we shall see, the rate of increase was not as regular as that. All we have to consider, at this stage, is the percentage rise over a given period.

Can this rise in the total number of civil servants be accounted for except on the assumption that such a total must always rise by a law governing its growth? It might be urged at this point that the period under discussion

8

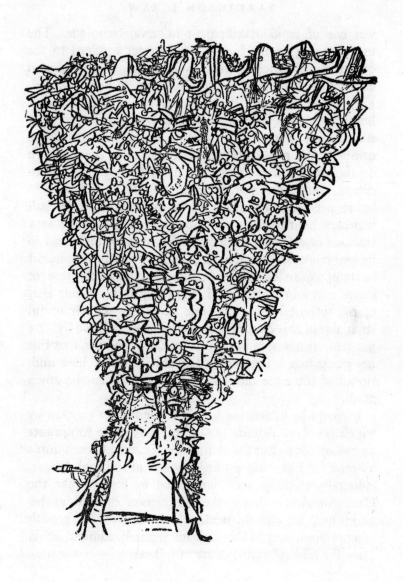

was one of rapid development in naval technique. The use of the flying machine was no longer confined to the eccentric. Electrical devices were being multiplied and elaborated. Submarines were tolerated if not approved. Engineer officers were beginning to be regarded as almost human. In so revolutionary an age we might expect that storekeepers would have more elaborate inventories to compile. We might not wonder to see more draughtsmen on the payroll, more designers, more technicians and scientists. But these, the dockyard officials, increased only by 40 per cent in number when the men of Whitehall increased their total by nearly 80 per cent. For every new foreman or electrical engineer at Portsmouth there had to be two more clerks at Charing Cross. From this we might be tempted to conclude, provisionally, that the rate of increase in administrative staff is likely to be double that of the technical staff at a time when the actually useful strength (in this case, of seamen) is being reduced by 31.5 per cent. It has been proved statistically, however, that this last percentage is irrelevant. The officials would have multiplied at the same rate had there been no actual seamen at all.

It would be interesting to follow the further progress by which the 8118 Admiralty staff of 1935 came to number 33,788 by 1954. But the staff of the Colonial Office affords a better field of study during a period of imperial decline. Admiralty statistics are complicated by factors (like the Fleet Air Arm) that make comparison difficult as between one year and the next. The Colonial Office growth is more significant in that it is more purely administrative. Here the relevant statistics are as follows:

1935	1939	1943	1947	1954
372	450	817	1139	1661

Before showing what the rate of increase is, we must observe that the extent of this department's responsibilities was far from constant during these twenty years. The colonial territories were not much altered in area or population between 1935 and 1939. They were considerably diminished by 1943, certain areas being in enemy hands. They were increased again in 1947, but have since then shrunk steadily from year to year as successive colonies achieve self-government. It would be rational to suppose that these changes in the scope of Empire would be reflected in the size of its central administration. But a glance at the figures is enough to convince us that the staff totals represent nothing but so many stages in an inevitable increase. And this increase, although related to that observed in other departments, has nothing to do with the size — or even the existence — of the Empire. What are the percentages of increase? We must ignore, for this purpose, the rapid increase in staff which accompanied the diminution of responsibility during World War II. We should note rather, the peacetime rates of increase: over 5.24 per cent between 1935 and 1939, and 6.55 per cent between 1947 and 1954. This gives an average increase of 5.89 per cent each year, a percentage markedly similar to that already found in the Admiralty staff increase between 1914 and 1928.

Further and detailed statistical analysis of departmental staffs would be inappropriate in such a work as this. It is hoped, however, to reach a tentative conclusion regarding the time likely to elapse between a given official's first appointment and the later appointment of his two or more assistants.

Dealing with the problem of pure staff accumulation, all our researches so far completed point to an average increase of 5.75 per cent per year. This fact established, it now becomes possible to state Parkinson's Law in mathematical form: In any public administrative department not actually at war, the staff increase may be expected to follow this formula —

$$x = \frac{2k^m + l}{n}$$

k is the number of staff seeking promotion through the appointment of subordinates; l represents the difference between the ages of appointment and retirement; m is the number of man-hours devoted to answering minutes within the department; and n is the number of effective units being administered. x will be the number of new staff required each year. Mathematicians will realize, of course, that to find the percentage increase they must multiply x by 100 and divide by the total of the previous year, thus:

$$\frac{100 \ (2k^m + l)}{yn} \ \%$$

where y represents the total original staff. This figure will invariably prove to be between 5.17 per cent and 6.56 per cent, irrespective of any variation in the amount of work (if any) to be done.

The discovery of this formula and of the general principles upon which it is based has, of course, no political
value. No attempt has been made to inquire whether departments *ought* to grow in size. Those who hold that this
growth is essential to gain full employment are fully entitled to their opinion. Those who doubt the stability of
an economy based upon reading each other's minutes are
equally entitled to theirs. It would probably be premature to
attempt at this stage any inquiry into the quantitative ratio
that should exist between the administrators and the administered. Granted, however, that a maximum ratio exists,
it should soon be possible to ascertain by formula how many
years will elapse before that ratio, in any given community,
will be reached. The forecasting of such a result will again
have no political value. Nor can it be sufficiently emphasized that Parkinson's Law is a purely scientific discovery,
inapplicable except in theory to the politics of the day. It
is not the business of the botanist to eradicate the weeds.
Enough for him if he can tell us just how fast they grow.

2

THE WILL OF THE PEOPLE
OR ANNUAL GENERAL MEETING

WE ARE ALL familiar with the basic difference between English and French parliamentary institutions; copied respectively by such other assemblies as derive from each. We all realize that this main difference has nothing to do with national temperament, but stems from their seating plans. The British, being brought up on team games, enter their House of Commons in the spirit of those who would rather be doing something else. If they cannot be playing golf or tennis, they can at least pretend that politics is a game with very similar rules. But for this device, Parliament would arouse even less interest than it does. So the British instinct is to form two opposing teams, with referee and linesmen, and let them debate until they exhaust themselves. The House of Commons is so arranged that the individual Member is practically compelled to take one side or the other before he knows what the arguments are, or even (in some cases) before he knows the subject of the dispute. His training from birth has been to play for his side, and this saves him from any undue mental effort. Sliding into a seat toward the end of a speech, he knows exactly how to take up the argument from the point it has reached. If the speaker is on his own side of the House, he will say "Hear, hear!" If he is on the opposite side, he can safely say "Shame!" or merely "Oh!" At some later stage he may have time to ask his neighbor what the debate is supposed to be about. Strictly speaking, however, there is no need for him to do this. He knows enough in any case not to kick into his own goal. The men who sit opposite

are entirely wrong and all their arguments are so much drivel. The men on his own side are statesmanlike, by contrast, and their speeches a singular blend of wisdom, eloquence, and moderation. Nor does it make the slightest difference whether he learned his politics at Harrow or in following the fortunes of Aston Villa. In either school he will have learned when to cheer and when to groan. But the British system depends entirely on its seating plan. If the benches did not face each other, no one could tell truth from falsehood — wisdom from folly — unless indeed by listening to it all. But to listen to it all would be ridiculous, for half the speeches must of necessity be nonsense.

In France the initial mistake was made of seating the representatives in a semicircle, all facing the chair. The resulting confusion could be imagined if it were not notorious. No real opposing teams could be formed and no one could tell (without listening) which argument was the more cogent. There was the further handicap of all the proceedings being in French — an example the United States wisely refused to follow. But the French system is bad enough even when the linguistic difficulty does not arise. Instead of having two sides, one in the right and the other in the wrong — so that the issue is clear from the outset — the French form a multitude of teams facing in all directions. With the field in such confusion, the game cannot even begin. Basically their representatives are of the Right or of the Left, according to where they sit. This is a perfectly sound scheme. The French have not gone to the extreme of seating people in alphabetical order. But the semicircular chamber allows of subtle distinctions between the various degrees of rightness and leftness. There is none of the clear-cut British distinction between rightness and wrongness. One deputy is described, politically, as to the left of Monsieur Untel but well to the right of Monsieur Quelquechose. What is anyone to make of that? What should we make of it even in English? What do they make of it themselves? The answer is, "Nothing."

All this is generally known. What is less generally recognized is that the paramount importance of the seating

16

plan applies to other assemblies and meetings, international, national, and local. It applies, moreover, to meetings round a table such as occur at a Round Table Conference. A moment's thought will convince us that a Square Table Conference would be something totally different and a Long Table Conference would be different again. These differences do not merely affect the length and acrimony of the discussion; they also affect what (if anything) is decided. Rarely, as we know, will the voting relate to the merits of the case. The final decision is influenced by a variety of factors, few of which need concern us at the moment. We should note, however, that the issue is actually *decided*, in the end, by the votes of the center bloc. This would not be true in the House of Commons, where no such bloc is allowed to develop. But at other conferences the center bloc is all important. This bloc essentially comprises the following elements:

a. Those who have failed to master any one of the memoranda written in advance and showered weeks beforehand on all those who are expected to be present.

b. Those who are too stupid to follow the proceedings at all. These are readily distinguishable by their tendency to mutter to each other: "What is the fellow talking about?"

c. Those who are deaf. They sit with their hands cupping their ears, growling "I wish people would speak up."

d. Those who were dead drunk in the small hours and have turned up (heaven knows why) with a splitting headache and a conviction that nothing matters either way.

e. The senile, whose chief pride is in being as fit as ever — fitter indeed than a lot of these younger men. "I

17

walked here," they whisper. "Pretty good for a man of eighty-two, what?"

f. The feeble, who have weakly promised to support both sides and don't know what to do about it. They are of two minds as to whether they should abstain from voting or pretend to be sick.

Toward capturing the votes of the center bloc the first step is to identify and count the members. That done, everything else depends on where they are to sit. The best technique is to detail off known and stalwart supporters to enter into conversation with named middle-bloc types before the meeting actually begins. In this preliminary chat the stalwarts will carefully avoid mentioning the main subject of debate. They will be trained to use the opening gambits listed below, corresponding to the categories *a* to *f*, into which the middle bloc naturally falls:

a. "Waste of time, I call it, producing all these documents. I have thrown most of mine away."

b. "I expect we shall be dazzled by eloquence before long. I often wish people would talk less and come to the point. They are too clever by half, if you ask me."

c. "The acoustics of this hall are simply terrible. You would have thought these scientific chaps could do something about it. For half the time I CAN'T HEAR WHAT IS BEING SAID. CAN YOU?"

d. "What a rotten place to meet! I think there is something the matter with the ventilation. It makes me feel almost unwell. What about you?"

e. "My goodness, I don't know how you do it! Tell me the secret. Is it what you have for breakfast?"

f. "There's so much to be said on both sides of the

question that I really don't know which side to support. What do you feel about it?"

If these gambits are correctly played, each stalwart will start a lively conversation, in the midst of which he will steer his middle-blocsman toward the forum. As he does this, another stalwart will place himself just *ahead* of the pair and moving in the same direction. The drill is best illustrated by a concrete example. We will suppose that stalwart X (Mr. Sturdy) is steering middle-blocsman Y (Mr. Waverley, type f) toward a seat *near the front*. Ahead goes stalwart Z (Mr. Staunch), who presently takes a seat without appearing to notice the two men following him. Staunch turns in the opposite direction and waves to someone in the distance. Then he leans over to make a few remarks to the man in front of him. Only when Waverley has sat down will Staunch presently turn toward him and say, "My dear fellow — how nice to see you!" Only some minutes later again will he catch sight of Sturdy and start visibly with surprise. "Hallo, Sturdy — I didn't think you would be here!" "I've recovered now," replies Sturdy. "It was only a chill." The seating order is thus made to appear completely accidental, casual, and friendly. That completes Phase I of the operation, and it would be much the same whatever the exact category in which the middle-blocsman is believed to fall.

Phase II has to be adjusted according to the character of the man to be influenced. In the case of Waverley (Type f) the object in Phase II is to avoid any discussion of the matter at issue but to produce the impression that the thing is already decided. Seated near the front, Waverley will be unable to see much of the other members and can be given the impression that they practically all think alike.

"Really," says Sturdy, "I don't know why I bothered to come. I gather that Item Four is pretty well agreed. All the fellows I meet seem to have made up their minds to vote for it." (Or against it, as the case may be.)

"Curious," says Staunch. "I was just going to say the same thing. The issue hardly seems to be in doubt."

"I had not really made up my own mind," says Sturdy.

"There was much to be said on either side. But opposition would really be a waste of time. What do you think, Waverley?"

"Well," says Waverley, "I must admit that I find the question rather baffling. On the one hand, there is good reason to agree to the motion . . . As against that . . . Do you think it will pass?"

"My dear Waverley, I would trust your judgment in this. You were saying just now that it is already agreed."

"Oh, was I? Well, there does seem to be a majority. . . . Or perhaps I should say . . . "

"Thank you, Waverley," says Staunch, "for your opinion. I think just the same but am particularly interested to find you agree with me. There is no one whose opinion I value more."

Sturdy, meanwhile, is leaning over to talk to someone in the row behind. What he actually says, in a low voice, is this, "How is your wife now? Is she out of hospital?" When he turns back again, however, it is to announce that the people behind all think the same. The motion is as good as passed. And so it is if the drill goes according to plan.

While the other side has been busy preparing speeches and phrasing amendments, the side with the superior technique will have concentrated on pinning each middle-blocsman between two reliable supporters. When the crucial moment comes, the raising of a hand on either side will practically compel the waverer to follow suit. Should he be actually asleep, as often happens with middle-blocsman in categories d and e, his hand will be raised for him by the member on his right. This rule is merely to obviate both his hands being raised, a gesture that has been known to attract unfavorable comment. With the middle bloc thus secured, the motion will be carried with a comfortable margin; or else rejected, if that is thought preferable. In nearly every matter of controversy to be decided by the will of the people, we can assume that the people who will decide are members of the middle bloc. Delivery of speeches is therefore a waste of time. The one party will never agree and the other party has agreed

22

already. Remains the middle bloc, the members of which divide into those who cannot hear what is being said and those who would not understand it even if they did. To secure their votes what is needed is primarily the example of others voting on either side of them. Their votes can thus be swayed by accident. How much better, by contrast, to sway them by design!

3

HIGH FINANCE
OR THE POINT OF VANISHING INTEREST

PEOPLE WHO understand high finance are of two kinds: those who have vast fortunes of their own and those who have nothing at all. To the actual millionaire a million dollars is something real and comprehensible. To the applied mathematician and the lecturer in economics (assuming both to be practically starving) a million dollars is at least as real as a thousand, they having never possessed either sum. But the world is full of people who fall between these two categories, knowing nothing of millions but well accustomed to think in thousands, and it is of these that finance committees are mostly comprised. The result is a phenomenon that has often been observed but never yet investigated. It might be termed the Law of Triviality. Briefly stated, it means that the time spent on any item of the agenda will be in inverse proportion to the sum involved.

On second thoughts, the statement that this law has never been investigated is not entirely accurate. Some work has actually been done in this field, but the investigators pursued a line of inquiry that led them nowhere. They assumed that the greatest significance should attach to the order in which items of the agenda are taken. They assumed, further, that most of the available time will be spent on items one to seven and that the later items will be allowed automatically to pass. The result is well known. The derision with which Dr. Guggenheim's lecture was received at the Muttworth Conference may have been thought excessive at the time, but all further discussions on this topic have tended to show that his critics were right. Years had been wasted in a research of which the basic assumptions were wrong. We realize now that position on the agenda is a minor consideration, so far, at least, as this problem is concerned. We consider also that Dr. Guggenheim was lucky to escape as he did, in his underwear. Had he dared to put his lame conclusions before the later conference in September, he would have faced something more than derision. The view would have been taken that he was deliberately wasting time.

If we are to make further progress in this investigation we must ignore all that has so far been done. We must start at the beginning and understand fully the way in which a finance committee actually works. For the sake of the general reader this can be put in dramatic form thus:

Chairman   We come now to Item Nine. Our Treasurer, Mr. McPhail, will report.

Mr. McPhail   The estimate for the Atomic Reactor is before you, sir, set forth in Appendix H of the subcommittee's report. You will see that the general design and layout has been approved by Professor McFission. The total cost will amount to $10,000,000. The contractors, Messrs. Mc-Nab and McHash, consider that the work should be complete by April, 1959. Mr. McFee, the consulting engineer, warns us that we should not count on completion before October, at the earliest. In this view he is supported by Dr. McHeap, the well-known geophysicist, who refers to the probable need for piling at the lower end of the site. The plan of the main building is before you — see Appendix IX — and the blueprint is laid on the table. I shall be glad to give any further information that members of this committee may require.

Chairman   Thank you, Mr. McPhail, for your very lucid explanation of the plan as proposed. I will now invite the members present to give us their views.

It is necessary to pause at this point and consider what views the members are likely to have. Let us suppose that they number eleven, including the Chairman but excluding the Secretary. Of these eleven members, four — including the chairman — do not know what a reactor is. Of the remainder, three do not know what it is for. Of those who know its purpose, only two have the least idea of what it should cost. One of these is Mr. Isaacson, the other is Mr. Brickworth. Either is in a position to say something. We may suppose that Mr. Isaacson is the first to speak.

Mr. Isaacson   Well, Mr. Chairman. I could wish that I felt more confidence in our contractors and consultant. Had we gone to Professor Levi in the first instance, and had the contract been given to Messrs. David and Goliath, I should have been happier about the whole scheme. Mr. Lyon-Daniels would not have wasted our time with wild guesses about the possible delay in completion, and Dr.

Moses Bullrush would have told us definitely whether piling would be wanted or not.

Chairman   I am sure we all appreciate Mr. Isaacson's anxiety to complete this work in the best possible way. I feel, however, that it is rather late in the day to call in new technical advisers. I admit that the main contract has still to be signed, but we have already spent very large sums. If we reject the advice for which we have paid, we shall have to pay as much again.
(*Other members murmur agreement.*)

Mr. Isaacson   I should like my observation to be minuted.

Chairman   Certainly. Perhaps Mr. Brickworth also has something to say on this matter?

Now Mr. Brickworth is almost the only man there who knows what he is talking about. There is a great deal he could say. He distrusts that round figure of $10,000,000. Why should it come out to exactly that? Why need they demolish the old building to make room for the new approach? Why is so large a sum set aside for "contingencies"? And who is McHeap, anyway? Is he the man who was sued last year by the Trickle and Driedup Oil Corporation? But Brickworth does not know where to begin. The other members could not read the blueprint if he referred to it. He would have to begin by explaining what a reactor is and no one there would admit that he did not already know. Better to say nothing.

Mr. Brickworth   I have no comment to make.

Chairman   Does any other member wish to speak? Very well. I may take it then that the plans and estimates are approved? Thank you. May I now sign the main contract on your behalf? *(Murmur of agreement)* Thank you. We can now move on to Item Ten.

Allowing a few seconds for rustling papers and unrolling diagrams, the time spent on Item Nine will have been just two minutes and a half. The meeting is going well. But some members feel uneasy about Item Nine. They wonder inwardly whether they have really been pulling their weight. It is too late to query that reactor scheme, but they would like to demonstrate, before the meeting ends, that they are alive to all that is going on.

Chairman   Item Ten. Bicycle shed for the use of the clerical staff. An estimate has been received from Messrs. Bodger and Woodworm, who undertake to complete the work for the sum of $2350. Plans and specification are before you, gentlemen.

Mr. Softleigh   Surely, Mr. Chairman, this sum is excessive. I note that the roof is to be of aluminum. Would not asbestos be cheaper?

Mr. Holdfast   I agree with Mr. Softleigh about the cost, but the roof should, in my opinion, be of galvanized iron. I incline to think that the shed could be built for $2000, or even less.

Mr. Daring   I would go further, Mr. Chairman. I question whether this shed is really necessary. We do too much for our staff as it is. They are never satisfied, that is the trouble. They will be wanting garages next.

Mr. Holdfast   No, I can't support Mr. Daring on this occasion. I think that the shed is needed. It is a question of material and cost . . .

The debate is fairly launched. A sum of $2350 is well within everybody's comprehension. Everyone can visualize a bicycle shed. Discussion goes on, therefore, for forty-five minutes, with the possible result of saving some $300. Members at length sit back with a feeling of achievement.

Chairman   Item Eleven. Refreshments supplied at meetings of the Joint Welfare Committee. Monthly, $4.75.

Mr. Softleigh   What type of refreshment is supplied on these occasions?

Chairman   Coffee, I understand.

Mr. Holdfast   And this means an annual charge of — let me see — $57?

Chairman   That is so.

Mr. Daring   Well, really, Mr. Chairman. I question whether this is justified. How long do these meetings last?

Now begins an even more acrimonious debate. There may be members of the committee who might fail to distinguish between asbestos and galvanized iron, but every man there knows about coffee — what it is, how it should be made, where it should be bought — and whether indeed it should be bought at all. This item on the agenda will occupy the members for an hour and a quarter, and they will end by asking the Secretary to procure further information, leaving the matter to be decided at the next meeting.

It would be natural to ask at this point whether a still smaller sum — $20, perhaps, or $10 — would occupy the Finance Committee for a proportionately longer time. On this point, it must be admitted, we are still ignorant. Our tentative conclusion must be that there is a point at which the whole tendency is reversed, the committee members

concluding that the sum is beneath their notice. Research has still to establish the point at which this reversal occurs. The transition from the $50 debate (an hour and a quarter) to the $20 debate (two and a half minutes) is indeed an abrupt one. It would be the more interesting to establish the exact point at which it occurs. More than that, it would be of practical value. Supposing, for example, that the point of vanishing interest is represented by the sum of $35, the Treasurer with an item of $62.80 on the agenda might well decide to present it as two items, one of $30.00 and the other of $32.80, with an evident saving in time and effort.

Conclusions at this juncture can be merely tentative, but there is some reason to suppose that the point of vanishing interest represents the sum the individual committee member is willing to lose on a bet or subscribe to a charity. An inquiry on these lines conducted on racecourses and in Methodist chapels, might go far toward solving the problem. Far greater difficulty may be encountered in attempting to discover the exact point at which the sum involved becomes too large to discuss at all. One thing apparent, however, is that the time spent on $10,000,000 and on $10 may well prove to be the same. The present estimated time of two and a half minutes is by no means exact, but there is clearly a space of time — something between two and four and a half minutes — which suffices equally for the largest and the smallest sums.

Much further investigation remains to be done, but the final results, when published, cannot fail to be of absorbing interest and of immediate value to mankind.

4

DIRECTORS AND COUNCILS
OR COEFFICIENT OF INEFFICIENCY

THE LIFE CYCLE of the committee is so basic to our knowledge of current affairs that it is surprising more attention has not been paid to the science of comitology. The first and most elementary principle of this science is that a committee is organic rather than mechanical in its nature: it is not a structure but a plant. It takes root and grows, it flowers, wilts, and dies, scattering the seed from which other committees will bloom in their turn. Only those who bear this principle in mind can make real headway in understanding the structure and history of modern government.

Committees, it is nowadays accepted, fall broadly into two categories, those (a) from which the individual member has something to gain; and those (b) to which the individual member merely has something to contribute. Examples of the B group, however, are relatively unimportant for our purpose; indeed some people doubt whether they are committees at all. It is from the more robust A group that we can learn most readily the principles which are common (with modifications) to all. Of the A group the most deeply rooted and luxuriant committees are those which confer the most power and prestige upon their members. In most parts of the world these committees are called "cabinets." This chapter is based on an extensive study of national cabinets, over space and time.

When first examined under the microscope, the cabinet council usually appears — to comitologists, historians, and even to the people who appoint cabinets — to consist ideally of five. With that number the plant is viable, allowing for two members to be absent or sick at any one time. Five members are easy to collect and, when collected, can act

with competence, secrecy, and speed. Of these original members four may well be versed, respectively, in finance, foreign policy, defense, and law. The fifth, who has failed to master any of these subjects, usually becomes the chairman or prime minister.

Whatever the apparent convenience might be of restricting the membership to five, however, we discover by observation that the total number soon rises to seven or nine. The usual excuse given for this increase, which is almost invariable (exceptions being found, however, in Luxembourg and Honduras), is the need for special knowledge on more than four topics. In fact, however, there is another and more potent reason for adding to the team. For in a cabinet of nine it will be found that policy is made by three, information supplied by two, and financial warning uttered by one. With the neutral chairman, that accounts for seven, the other two appearing at first glance to be merely ornamental. This allocation of duties was first noted in Britain in about 1639, but there can be no doubt that the folly of including more than three able and talkative men in one committee had been discovered long before then. We know little as yet about the function of the two silent members but we have good reason to believe that a cabinet, in this second stage of development, might be unworkable without them.

There are cabinets in the world (those of Costa Rica, Ecuador, Northern Ireland, Liberia, the Philippines, Uruguay, and Panama will at once be called to mind) which have remained in this second stage — that is, have restricted their membership to nine. These remain, however, a small minority. Elsewhere and in larger territories cabinets have generally been subject to a law of growth. Other members come to be admitted, some with a claim to special knowledge but more because of their nuisance value when excluded. Their opposition can be silenced only by implicating them in every decision that is made. As they are brought in (and placated) one after another, the total membership rises from ten toward twenty. In this third stage of cabinets, there are already considerable drawbacks.

The most immediately obvious of these disadvantages is the difficulty of assembling people at the same place, date, and time. One member is going away on the 18th, whereas another does not return until the 21st. A third is never free on Tuesdays, and a fourth never available before 5 P.M. But that is only the beginning of the trouble, for, once most of them are collected, there is a far greater chance of members proving to be elderly, tiresome, inaudible, and deaf. Relatively few were chosen from any idea that they are or could be or have ever been useful. A majority perhaps were brought in merely to conciliate some outside group. Their tendency is therefore to report what happens to the group they represent. All secrecy is lost and, worst of all, members begin to prepare their speeches. They address the meeting and tell their friends afterwards about what they imagine they have said. But the more these merely representative members assert themselves, the more loudly do other outside groups clamor for representation. Internal parties form and seek to gain strength by further recruitment. The total of twenty is reached and passed. And thereby, quite suddenly, the cabinet enters the fourth and final stage of its history.

For at this point of cabinet development (between 20 and 22 members) the whole committee suffers an abrupt organic or chemical change. The nature of this change is easy to trace and comprehend. In the first place, the five members who matter will have taken to meeting beforehand. With decisions already reached, little remains for

37

the nominal executive to do. And, as a consequence of this, all resistance to the committee's expansion comes to an end. More members will not waste more time; for the whole meeting is, in any case, a waste of time. So the pressure of outside groups is temporarily satisfied by the admission of their representatives, and decades may elapse before they realize how illusory their gain has been. With the doors wide open, membership rises from 20 to 30, from 30 to 40. There may soon be an instance of such a membership reaching the thousand mark. But this does not matter. For the cabinet has already ceased to be a real cabinet, and has been succeeded in its old functions by some other body.

Five times in English history the plant has moved through its life cycle. It would admittedly be difficult to prove that the first incarnation of the cabinet — the English Council of the Crown, now called the House of Lords — ever had a membership as small as five. When we first hear of it, indeed, its more intimate character had already been lost, with a hereditary membership varying from 29 to 50. Its subsequent expansion, however, kept pace with its loss of power. In round figures, it had 60 members in 1601, 140 in 1661, 220 in 1760, 400 in 1850, 650 in 1911, and 850 in 1952.

At what point in this progression did the inner committee appear in the womb of the peerage? It appeared in about 1257, its members being called the Lords of the King's Council and numbering less than 10. They numbered no more than 11 in 1378, and as few still in 1410. Then, from the reign of Henry V, they began to multiply. The 20 of 1433 had become the 41 of 1504, the total reaching 172 before the council finally ceased to meet.

Within the King's Council there developed the cabinet's third incarnation — the Privy Council — with an original membership of nine. It rose to 20 in 1540, to 29 in 1547, and to 44 in 1558. The Privy Council as it ceased to be effective increased proportionately in size. It had 47 members in 1679, 67 in 1723, 200 in 1902, and 300 in 1951.

Within the Privy Council there developed the junto or Cabinet Council, which effectively superseded the former in about 1615. Numbering 8 when we first hear of it, its members had come to number 12 by about 1700, and 20 by 1725. The Cabinet Council was then superseded in about 1740 by an inner group, since called simply the Cabinet. Its development is best studied in tabular form. This is shown in Table I.

TABLE I – GROWTH OF THE ENGLISH CABINET

1740	5	1885	16	1945	16
1784	7	1900	20	1945	20
1801	12	1915	22	1949	17
1841	14	1935	22	1954	18
		1939	23		

From 1939, it will be apparent, there has been a struggle to save this institution; a struggle similar to the attempts made to save the Privy Council during the reign of Queen Elizabeth I. The Cabinet appeared to be in its decline in 1940, with an inner cabinet (of 5, 7, or 9 members) ready to take its place. The issue, however, remains in doubt. It is just possible that the British cabinet is still an important body.

Compared with the cabinet of Britain, the cabinet of the

United States has shown an extraordinary resistance to political inflation. It had the appropriate number of 5 members in 1789, still only 7 by 1840, 9 by 1901, 10 by 1913, 11 by 1945, and then — against tradition — had come down to 10 again by 1953. Whether this attempt, begun in 1947, to restrict the membership will succeed for long is doubtful. All experience would suggest the inevitability of the previous trend. In the meanwhile, the United States enjoys (with Guatemala and El Salvador) a reputation for cabinet-exclusiveness, having actually fewer cabinet ministers than Nicaragua or Paraguay.

How do other countries compare in this respect? The majority of non-totalitarian countries have cabinets that number between 12 and 20 members. Taking the average

TABLE II – SIZE OF CABINETS

No. of Members		No. of Members	
6	Honduras, Luxembourg	16	Iraq, Netherlands, Turkey
7	Haiti, Iceland, Switzerland	17	Eire, Israel, Spain
		18	Egypt, Gt. Britain, Mexico
9	Costa Rica, Ecuador, N. Ireland, Liberia, Panama, Philippines, Uruguay	19	W. Germany, Greece, Indonesia, Italy
		20	Australia, Formosa, Japan
10	Guatemala, El Salvador, United States	21	Argentina, Burma, Canada, France
11	Brazil, Nicaragua, Pakistan, Paraguay	22	China
		24	E. Germany
12	Bolivia, Chile, Peru	26	Bulgaria
13	Colombia, Dominican R., Norway, Thailand	27	Cuba
		29	Rumania
14	Denmark, India, S. Africa, Sweden	32	Czechoslovakia
		35	Yugoslavia
15	Austria, Belgium, Finland, Iran, New Zealand, Portugal, Venezuela	38	USSR

of over 60 countries, we find that it comes to over 16; the most popular numbers are 15 (seven instances) and 9 (seven again). Easily the queerest cabinet is that of New Zealand, one member of which has to be announced as "Minister of Lands, Minister of Forests, Minister of Maori Affairs, Minister in charge of Maori Trust Office and of Scenery Preservation." The toastmaster at a New Zealand banquet must be equally ready to crave silence for "The Minister of Health, Minister Assistant to the Prime Minister, Minister in Charge of State Advances Corporation, Census, and Statistics Department, Public Trust Office and Publicity and Information." In other lands this oriental profusion is fortunately rare.

A study of the British example would suggest that the point of ineffectiveness in a cabinet is reached when the total membership exceeds 20 or perhaps 21. The Council of the Crown, the King's Council, the Privy Council had each passed the 20 mark when their decline began. The present British cabinet is just short of that number now, having recoiled from the abyss. We might be tempted to conclude from this that cabinets — or other committees — with a membership in excess of 21 are losing the reality of power and that those with a larger membership have already lost it. No such theory can be tenable, however, without statistical proof. Table II on the preceding page attempts to furnish part of it.

. Should we be justified in drawing a line in that table under the name of France (21 cabinet members) with an explanatory note to say that the cabinet is not the real power in countries shown below that line? Some comitologists would accept that conclusion without further research. Others emphasize the need for careful investigation, more especially around the borderline of 21. But that the coefficient of inefficiency must lie between 19 and 22 is now very generally agreed.

What tentative explanation can we offer for this hypothesis? Here we must distinguish sharply between fact and theory, between the symptom and the disease. About the most obvious symptom there is little disagreement. It is known that with over 20 members present a meeting begins to change character. Conversations develop separately at either end of the table. To make himself heard, the member has therefore to rise. Once on his feet, he cannot help making a speech, if only from force of habit. "Mr. Chairman," he will begin, "I think I may assert without fear of contradiction — and I am speaking now from twenty-five (I might almost say twenty-seven) years of experience — that we must view this matter in the gravest light. A heavy responsibility rests upon us, sir, and I for one . . ." Amid all this drivel the useful men present, if there are any, exchange little notes that read, "Lunch with me tomorrow — we'll fix it then."

What else can they do? The voice drones on interminably. The orator might just as well be talking in his sleep. The committee of which he is the most useless member has ceased to matter. It is finished. It is hopeless. It is dead.

So much is certain. But the root cause of the trouble goes deeper and has still, in part, to be explored. Too many vital factors are unknown. What is the shape and size of the table? What is the average age of those present? At what hour does the committee meet? In a book for the non-specialist it would be absurd to repeat the calculations by which the first and tentative coefficient of inefficiency has been reached. It should be enough to state that prolonged research at the Institute of Comitology has given rise to a formula which is now widely (although not universally) accepted by the experts in this field. It should perhaps be explained that the investigators assumed a temperate climate, leather-padded chairs and a high level of sobriety. On this basis, the formula is as follows:

$$x = \frac{m^\circ(a - d)}{y + p\sqrt{b}}$$

Where m = the average number of members actually present; ° = the number of members influenced by outside pressure groups; a = the average age of the members; d = the distance in centimeters between the two members who are seated farthest from each other; y = the number of years since the cabinet or committee was first formed; p = the patience of the chairman, as measured on the Peabody scale; b = the average blood pressure of the three oldest members, taken shortly before the time of meeting. Then x = the number of members effectively present at the moment when the efficient working of the cabinet or other committee has become manifestly impossible. This is the coefficient of inefficiency and it is found to lie between 19.9 and 22.4. (The decimals represent partial attendance; those absent for a part of the meeting.)

It would be unsound to conclude, from a cursory inspection of this equation that the science of comitology is in an advanced state of development. Comitologists and subcomitologists would make no such claim, if only from fear of unemployment. They emphasize, rather, that their studies have barely begun and that they are on the brink of astounding progress. Making every allowance for self-interest — which means discounting 90 per cent of what they say — we can safely assume that much work remains to do.

We should eventually be able, for example, to learn the formula by which the optimum number of committee members may be determined. Somewhere between the number of 3 (when a quorum is impossible to collect) and approximately 21 (when the whole organism begins to perish), there lies the golden number. The interesting theory has been propounded that this number must be 8. Why? Because it is the only number which all existing states (See Table II above) have agreed to avoid. Attractive as this theory may seem at first sight, it is open to one serious objection. Eight was the number preferred by King Charles I for his Committee of State. And look what happened to him!

5

THE SHORT LIST
OR PRINCIPLES OF SELECTION

A PROBLEM constantly before the modern administration, whether in government or business, is that of personnel selection. The inexorable working of Parkinson's Law ensures that appointments have constantly to be made and the question is always how to choose the right candidate from all who present themselves. In ascertaining the principles upon which the choice should be made, we may properly consider, under separate heads, the methods used in the past and the methods used at the present day.

Past methods, not entirely disused, fall into two main categories, the British and the Chinese. Both deserve careful consideration, if only for the reason that they were obviously more successful than any method now considered fashionable. The British method (old pattern) depended upon an interview in which the candidate had to establish his identity. He would be confronted by elderly gentlemen seated round a mahogany table who would presently ask him his name. Let us suppose that the candidate replied, "John Seymour." One of the gentlemen would then say, "Any relation of the Duke of Somerset?" To this the candidate would say, quite possibly, "No, sir." Then another gentleman would say, "Perhaps you are related, in that case, to the Bishop of Watminster?" If he said "No, sir" again, a third would ask in despair, "To whom then are you related?" In the event of the candidate's saying, "Well, my father is a fishmonger in Cheapside," the interview was virtually over. The members of the Board would exchange significant glances, one would press a bell and another tell the footman, "Throw this person out." One name could be crossed off the list without further discussion. Supposing the next candidate was Henry Molyneux and a nephew of the Earl of Sefton, his chances remained fair up to the moment when George Howard arrived and proved to be a grandson of the Duke of Norfolk. The Board encountered no serious difficulty until they had to compare the claims of the third son of a baronet with the second but illegitimate son of a viscount. Even then they could refer to a Book of Precedence. So their choice was made and often with the best results.

The Admiralty version of this British method (old pattern) was different only in its more restricted scope. The Board of Admirals were unimpressed by titled relatives as such. What they sought to establish was a service connection. The ideal candidate would reply to the second question, "Yes, Admiral Parker is my uncle. My father is Captain Foley, my grandfather Commodore Foley. My mother's father was Admiral Hardy. Commander Hardy is my uncle. My eldest brother is a Lieutenant in the Royal Marines, my next brother is a cadet at Dartmouth and my younger brother wears a sailor suit." "Ah!" the senior Admiral would say. "And what made you think of joining the Navy?" The answer to this question, however, would

scarcely matter, the clerk present having already noted the candidate as acceptable. Given a choice between two candidates, both equally acceptable by birth, a member of the Board would ask suddenly, "What was the number of the taxi you came in?" The candidate who said "I came by bus" was then thrown out. The candidate who said, truthfully, "I don't know," was rejected, and the candidate who said "Number 2351" (lying) was promptly admitted to the service as a boy with initiative. This method often produced excellent results.

The British method (new pattern) was evolved in the late nineteenth century as something more suitable for a democratic country. The Selection Committee would ask briskly, "What school were you at?" and would be told Harrow, Haileybury, or, Rugby, as the case might be. "What games do you play?" would be the next and invariable question. A promising candidate would reply, "I have played tennis for England, cricket for Yorkshire, rugby for the Harlequins, and fives for Winchester." The next question would then be "Do you play polo?" — just to prevent the candidate's thinking too highly of himself. Even without playing polo, however, he was evidently worth serious consideration. Little time, by contrast, was wasted on the man who admitted to having been educated at Wiggleworth. "Where?" the chairman would ask in astonishment, and "Where's that?" after the name had been repeated. "Oh, in *Lancashire!*" he would say at last. Just for a matter of form, some member might ask, "What games do you play?" But the reply "Table tennis for Wigan, cycling for Blackpool, and snooker for Wiggleworth" would finally delete his name from the list. There might even be some muttered comment upon people who deliberately wasted the committee's time. Here again was a method which produced good results.

The Chinese method (old pattern) was at one time so extensively copied by other nations that few people realize its Chinese origin. This is the method of Competitive Written Examination. In China under the Ming Dynasty the more promising students used to sit for the provincial examination, held every third year. It lasted three sessions of three days each. During the first session the candidate wrote three essays and composed a poem of eight couplets. During the second session he wrote five essays on a classical theme. During the third, he wrote five essays on the art of government. The successful candidates (perhaps two per cent) then sat for their final examination at the imperial capital. It lasted only one session, the candidate writing one essay on a current political problem. Of those who were successful the majority were admitted to the civil service, the man with the highest marks being destined for the highest office. The system worked fairly well.

The Chinese system was studied by Europeans between 1815 and 1830 and adopted by the English East India Company in 1832. The effectiveness of this method was investigated by a committee in 1854, with Macaulay as chairman. The result was that the system of competitive examination was introduced into the British Civil Service in 1855. An essential feature of the Chinese examinations had been their literary character. The test was in a knowledge of the classics, in an ability to write elegantly (both prose and verse) and in the stamina necessary to complete the course. All these features were faithfully incorporated in the Trevelyan-Northcote Report, and thereafter in the system it did so much to create. It was assumed that classical learning and literary ability would fit any candidate for any administrative post. It was assumed (no doubt rightly) that a scientific education would fit a candidate for nothing — except, possibly, science. It was known, finally, that it is virtually impossible to find an order of merit among people who have been examined in different subjects. Since it is impracticable to decide whether one man is better in geology than another man in physics, it is at least convenient to be able to rule them both out as useless. When all candidates alike have to write Greek or Latin verse, it is relatively easy to decide which verse is the best. Men thus selected on their classical performance were then sent forth to govern India. Those with lower marks were retained to govern England. Those with still lower marks were rejected altogether or sent to the colonies. While it would be totally wrong to describe this system as a failure, no one could claim for it the success that had attended the systems hitherto in use. There was no guarantee, to begin with, that the man with the highest marks might not turn out to be off his head; as was sometimes found to be the case. Then again the writing of Greek verse might prove to be the sole accomplishment that some candidates had or would ever have. On occasion, a successful applicant may even have been impersonated at the examination by someone else, subsequently proving unable to write Greek verse when the occasion arose. Selection by competitive examination was never therefore more than a moderate success.

Whatever the faults, however, of the competitive written examination, it certainly produced better results than any method that has been attempted since. Modern methods center upon the intelligence test and the psychological interview. The defect in the intelligence test is that high marks are gained by those who subsequently prove to be practically illiterate. So much time has been spent in studying the art of being tested that the candidate has rarely had time for anything else. The psychological interview has developed today into what is known as ordeal by house party. The candidates spend a pleasant weekend under expert observation. As one of them trips over the doormat and says "Bother!" examiners lurking in the background whip out their notebooks and jot down, "Poor physical coordination" and "Lacks self-control." There is no need to describe this method in detail, but its results are all about us and are obviously deplorable. The persons who satisfy this type of examiner are usually of a cautious and suspicious temperament, pedantic and smug, saying little and doing nothing. It is quite common, when appointments are made by this method, for one man to be chosen from five hundred applicants, only to be sacked a few weeks later as useless even beyond the standards of his department. Of the various methods of selection so far tried, the latest is unquestionably the worst.

What method should be used in the future? A clue to a possible line of investigation is to be found in one little-publicized aspect of contemporary selective technique. So rarely does the occasion arise for appointing a Chinese translator to the Foreign Office or State Department that the method used is little known. The post is advertised and the applications go, let us suppose, to a committee of five. Three are civil servants and two are Chinese scholars of great eminence. Heaped on the table before this committee are 483 forms of application, with testimonials attached. All the applicants are Chinese and all without exception have a first degree from Peking or Amoy and a Doctorate of Philosophy from Cornell or Johns Hopkins. The majority of the candidates have at one time held ministerial office in Formosa. Some have attached their photographs. Others have (perhaps wisely) refrained from doing so. The chairman turns to the leading Chinese expert and says, "Perhaps Dr. Wu can tell us which of these candidates should be put on the short list." Dr. Wu smiles enigmatically and points to the heap. "None of them any good," he says briefly. "But how — I mean, why not?" asks the chairman, surprised. "Because no good scholar would ever apply. He would fear to lose face if he were not chosen." "So what do we do now?" asks the chairman. "I think," says Dr. Wu, "we might persuade Dr. Lim to take this post. What do you think, Dr. Lee?" "Yes, I think he might," says Lee, "but we couldn't approach him ourselves of course. We could ask Dr. Tan whether he thinks Dr. Lim would be interested." "I don't know Dr. Tan," says Wu, "but I know his friend Dr. Wong." By then the chairman is too muddled to know who is to be approached by whom. But the great thing is that all the applications are thrown into the waste-paper basket, only one candidate being considered, and he a man who did not apply.

We do not advise the universal adoption of the modern Chinese method but we draw from it the useful conclusion that the failure of other methods is mainly due to there being too many candidates. There are, admittedly, some initial steps by which the total may be reduced. The formula "Reject everyone over 50 or under 20 plus everyone called Murphy" is now universally used, and its application will somewhat reduce the list. The names remaining will still, however, be too numerous. To choose between three hundred people, all well qualified and highly recommended, is not really possible. We are driven therefore to conclude that the mistake lies in the original advertisement. It has attracted too many applications. The disadvantage of this is so little realized that people devise advertisements in terms which will inevitably attract thousands. A post of responsibility is announced as vacant, the previous occupant being now in the Senate or the House of Lords. The salary is large, the pension generous, the duties nominal, the privileges immense, the perquisites valuable, free residence provided with official car and unlimited facilities for travel. Candidates should apply, promptly but carefully, enclosing copies (not originals) of not more than three recent testimonials. What is the result? A deluge of applications, many from lunatics and as many again from retired army majors with a gift (as they always claim) for handling men. There is nothing to do except burn the lot and start thinking all over again. It would have saved time and trouble to do some thinking in the first place.

Only a little thought is needed to convince us that the perfect advertisement would attract only one reply and that from the right man. Let us begin with an extreme example.

Wanted — Acrobat capable of crossing a slack wire 200 feet above raging furnace. Twice nightly, three times on Saturday.

Salary offered £25 (or $70 U.S.) per week. No pension and no compensation in the event of injury. Apply in person at Wildcat Circus between the hours of 9 A.M. and 10 A.M.

The wording of this may not be perfect but the aim should be so to balance the inducement in salary against the possible risks involved that only a single applicant will appear. It is needless to ask for details of qualifications and experience. No one unskilled on the slack wire would find the offer attractive. It is needless to insist that candidates should be physically fit, sober, and free from fits of dizziness. They know that. It is just as needless to stipulate that those nervous of heights need not apply. They won't. The skill of the advertiser consists in adjusting the salary to the danger. An offer of £1000 (or $3000 U.S.) per week might produce a dozen applicants. An offer of £15 (or $35 U.S.) might produce none. Somewhere between those two figures lies the exact sum to specify, the minimum figure to attract anyone actually capable of doing the job. If there is more than one applicant, the figure has been placed a trifle too high.

Let us now take, for comparison, a less extreme example.

Wanted — An archaeologist with high academic qualifications willing to spend fifteen years in excavating the Inca tombs at Helsdump on the Alligator River. Knighthood or equivalent honor guaranteed. Pension payable but never yet claimed. Salary of £2000 (or $6000 U.S.) per year. Apply in triplicate to the Director of the Grubbenburrow Institute, Sickdale, Ill., U.S.A.

Here the advantages and drawbacks are neatly balanced. There is no need to insist that candidates must be patient, tough, intrepid, and single. The terms of the advertisement have eliminated all who are not. It is unnecessary to require that candidates must be mad on excavating tombs. Mad is just what they will certainly be. Having thus reduced the possible applicants to a maximum of about three, the terms of the advertisement place the salary just too low to attract two of them and the promised honor *just* high enough to interest the third. We may suppose that, in this case, the offer of a K.C.M.G. would have produced two applications, the offer of an O.B.E., none. The result is a single candidate. He is off his head but that does not matter. He is the man we want.

It may be thought that the world offers comparatively few opportunities to appoint slack-wire acrobats and tomb excavators, and that the problem is more often to find candidates for less exotic appointments. This is true, but the same principles can be applied. Their application demands, however — as is evident — a greater degree of skill. Let us suppose that the post to be filled is that of Prime Minister. The modern tendency is to trust in various methods of election, with results that are almost invariably disastrous. Were we to turn, instead, to the fairy stories we learned in childhood, we should realize that at the period to which these stories relate far more satisfactory methods were in use. When the king had to choose a man to marry his eldest or only daughter and so inherit the kingdom, he normally planned some obstacle course from which only the right candidate would emerge with credit; and from which indeed (in many instances) only the right candidate would emerge at all. For imposing such a test the kings of that rather vaguely defined period were well provided with both personnel and equipment. Their establishment included magicians, demons, fairies, vampires, werewolves, giants, and dwarfs. Their territories were supplied with magic mountains, rivers of fire, hidden treasures, and enchanted forests. It might be urged that modern governments are in this respect less fortunate. This, however, is by no means certain. An administrator able to command the services of psychologists, psychiatrists, alienists, statisticians, and efficiency experts is not perhaps in a worse (or better) position than one relying upon hideous crones and fairy godmothers. An administration equipped with movie cameras, television apparatus, radio networks, and X-ray machines would not appear to be in a worse (or better) position than one employing magic wands, crystal balls, wishing wells, and cloaks of invisibility. Their means of assessment would seem, at any rate, to be strictly comparable. All that is required is to translate the technique of the fairy story into a form applicable to the modern world. In this, as we shall see, there is no essential difficulty.

The first step in the process is to decide on the qualities a Prime Minister ought to have. These need not be the same in all circumstances, but they need to be listed and agreed upon. Let us suppose that the qualities deemed essential are (1) Energy, (2) Courage, (3) Patriotism, (4) Experience, (5) Popularity, and (6) Eloquence. Now, it will be observed that all these are general qualities which all possible applicants would believe themselves to possess. The field could readily, of course, be narrowed by stipulating (4) Experience of lion-taming, or (6) Eloquence in Mandarin. But that is not the way in which we want to narrow the field. We do not want to stipulate a quality in a special form; rather, each quality in an exceptional degree. In other words, the successful candidate must be the most energetic, courageous, patriotic, experienced, popular, and eloquent man in the country. Only one man can answer to that description and his is the only application we want. The terms of the appointment must thus be phrased so as to exclude everyone else. We should therefore word the advertisement in some such way as follows:

Wanted — Prime Minister of Ruritania. Hours of work: 4 A.M. to 11.59 P.M. Candidates must be prepared to fight three rounds with the current heavyweight champion (regulation gloves to be worn). Candidates will die for their country, by painless means, on reaching the age of retirement (65). They will have to pass an examination in parliamentary procedure and will be liquidated should they fail to obtain 95% marks. They will also be liquidated if they fail to gain 75% votes in a popularity poll held under the Gallup Rules. They will finally be invited to try their eloquence on a Baptist Congress, the object being to induce those present to rock and roll. Those who fail will be liquidated. All candidates should present themselves at the Sporting Club (side entrance) at 11.15 A.M. on the morning of September 19. Gloves will be provided, but they should bring their own rubber-soled shoes, singlet, and shorts.

Observe that this advertisement saves all trouble about application forms, testimonials, photographs, references, and short lists. If the advertisement has been correctly worded, there will be only one applicant, and he can take office immediately — well, almost immediately. But what if there is no applicant? That is proof that the advertisement needs rewording. We have evidently asked for something more than exists. So the same advertisement (which is, after all, quite economical in space) can be inserted again with some slight adjustment. The pass mark in the examination can be reduced to 85 per cent with 65 per cent of the votes required in the popularity poll, and only two rounds against the heavyweight. Conditions can be successively relaxed, indeed, until an applicant appears.

Suppose, however, that two or even three candidates present themselves. We shall know that we have been insufficiently scientific. It may be that the pass mark in the examination has been too abruptly lowered — it should have been 87 per cent, perhaps, with 66 per cent in the popularity poll. Whatever the cause, the damage has been done. Two, or possibly three, candidates are in the waiting room. We have a choice to make and cannot waste all the morning on it. One policy would be to start the ordeal and eliminate the candidates who emerge with least credit. There is, nevertheless, a quicker way. Let us assume that all three candidates have all the qualities already defined as essential. The only thing we need do is add one further quality and apply the simplest test of all. To do this, we ask the nearest young lady (receptionist or stenographer, as the case may be), "Which would you prefer?" She will promptly point out one of the candidates and so finish the matter. It has been objected that this procedure is the same thing as tossing a coin or otherwise letting chance decide. There is, in fact, no element of chance. It is merely the last-minute insistence on one other quality, one not so far taken into account: the quality of sex appeal.

6

PLANS AND PLANTS
OR THE ADMINISTRATION BLOCK

EVERY STUDENT of human institutions is familiar with the standard test by which the importance of the individual may be assessed. The number of doors to be passed, the number of his personal assistants, the number of his telephone receivers — these three figures, taken with the depth of his carpet in centimeters, have given us a simple formula that is reliable for most parts of the world. It is less widely known that the same sort of measurement is applicable, *but in reverse*, to the institution itself.

Take, for example, a publishing organization. Publishers have a strong tendency, as we know, to live in a state of chaotic squalor. The visitor who applies at the obvious entrance is led outside and around the block, down an alley and up three flights of stairs. A research establishment is similarly housed, as a rule, on the ground floor of what was once a private house, a crazy wooden corridor leading thence to a corrugated iron hut in what was once the garden. Are we not all familiar, moreover, with the layout of an international airport? As we emerge from the aircraft, we see (over to our right or left) a lofty structure wrapped in scaffolding. Then the air hostess leads us into a hut with an asbestos roof. Nor do we suppose for a moment that it will ever be otherwise. By the time the permanent building is complete the airfield will have been moved to another site.

The institutions already mentioned — lively and productive as they may be — flourish in such shabby and makeshift surroundings that we might turn with relief to an institution clothed from the outset with convenience and dignity. The outer door, in bronze and glass, is placed centrally in a symmetrical façade. Polished shoes glide quietly over shining rubber to the glittering and silent elevator. The overpoweringly cultured receptionist will murmer with carmine lips into an ice-blue receiver. She will wave you into a chromium armchair, consoling you with a dazzling smile for any slight but inevitable delay. Looking up from a glossy magazine, you will observe how the wide corridors radiate toward departments A, B, and C. From behind closed doors will come the subdued noise of an ordered activity. A minute later and you are ankle deep in the director's carpet, plodding sturdily toward his distant, tidy desk. Hypnotized by the chief's unwavering stare, cowed by the Matisse hung upon his wall, you will feel that you have found real efficiency at last.

In point of fact you will have discovered nothing of the kind. It is now known that a perfection of planned layout is achieved only by institutions on the point of collapse. This apparently paradoxical conclusion is based upon a wealth of archaeological and historical research, with the more esoteric details of which we need not concern ourselves. In general principle, however, the method pursued has been to select and date the buildings which appear to have been perfectly designed for their purpose. A study and comparison of these has tended to prove that perfection of planning is a sympton of decay. During a period of exciting discovery or progress there is no time to plan the perfect headquarters. The time for that comes later, when all the important work has been done. Perfection, we know, is finality; and finality is death.

Thus, to the casual tourist, awestruck in front of St. Peter's, Rome, the Basilica and the Vatican must seem the ideal setting for the Papal Monarchy at the very height of its prestige and power. Here, he reflects, must Innocent III have thundered his anathema. Here must Gregory VII have laid down the law. But a glance at the guidebook will convince the traveler that the really powerful Popes reigned long before the present dome was raised, and reigned not infrequently somewhere else. More than that, the later Popes lost half their authority while the work was still in progress. Julius II, whose decision it was to build, and Leo X, who approved Raphael's design, were dead long before the buildings assumed their present shape. Bramante's palace was still building until 1565, the great church not consecrated until 1626, nor the piazza colonnades finished until 1667. The great days of the Papacy were over before the perfect setting was even planned. They were almost forgotten by the date of its completion.

That this sequence of events is in no way exceptional can be proved with ease. Just such a sequence can be found in the history of the League of Nations. Great hopes centered on the League from its inception in 1920 until about 1930. By 1933, at the latest, the experiment was seen to have failed. Its physical embodiment, however, the Palace

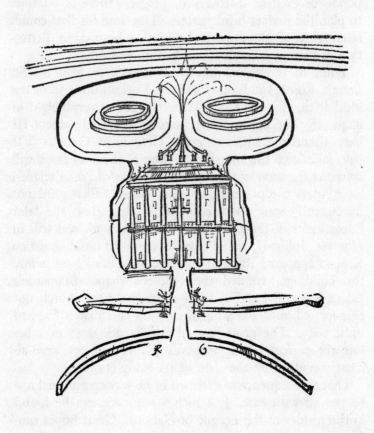

of the Nations, was not opened until 1937. It was a structure no doubt justly admired. Deep thought had gone into the design of secretariat and council chambers, committee rooms and cafeteria. Everything was there which ingenuity could devise — except, indeed, the League itself. By the year when its Palace was formally opened the League had practically ceased to exist.

It might be urged that the Palace of Versailles is an instance of something quite opposite; the architectural embodiment of Louis XIV's monarchy at its height. But here again the facts refuse to fit the theory. For granted that Versailles may typify the triumphant spirit of the age, it was mostly completed very late in the reign, and some of it indeed during the reign that followed. The building of Versailles mainly took place between 1669 and 1685. The king did not move there until 1682, and even then the work was still in progress. The famous royal bedroom was not occupied until 1701, nor the chapel finished until nine years later. Considered as a seat of government, as apart from a royal residence, Versailles dates in part from as late as 1756. As against that, Louis XIV's real triumphs were mostly before 1679, the apex of his career reached in 1682 itself and his power declining from about 1685. According to one historian, Louis, in coming to Versailles "was already sealing the doom of his line and race." Another says of Versailles that "The whole thing . . . was completed just when the decline of Louis's power had begun." A third tacitly supports this theory by describing the period 1685–1713 as "The Years of Decline." In other words, the visitor who thinks Versailles the place from which Turenne rode forth to victory is essentially mistaken. It would be historically more correct to picture the embarrassment, in that setting, of those who came with the news of defeat at Blenheim. In a palace resplendent with emblems of victory they can hardly have known which way to look.

Mention of Blenheim must naturally call to mind the palace of that name built for the victorious Duke of Marlborough. Here again we have a building ideally planned, this time as the place of retirement for a national hero. Its heroic proportions are more dramatic perhaps than convenient, but the general effect is just what the architects intended. No scene could more fittingly enshrine a legend. No setting could have been more appropriate for the meeting of old comrades on the anniversary of a battle. Our pleasure, however, in picturing the scene is spoiled by our realization that it cannot have taken place. The Duke never lived there and never even saw it finished. His actual residence was at Holywell, near St. Alban's, and (when in town) at Marlborough House. He died at Windsor Lodge and his old comrades, when they held a reunion, are known to have dined in a tent. Blenheim took long in building, not because of the elaboration of the design — which was admittedly quite elaborate enough — but because the Duke was in disgrace and even, for two years, in exile during the period which might otherwise have witnessed its completion.

What of the monarchy which the Duke of Marlborough served? Just as tourists now wander, guidebook in hand, through the Orangerie or the Galerie des Glaces, so the future archaeologist may peer around what once was London. And he may well incline to see in the ruins of Buckingham Palace a true expression of British monarchy. He will trace the great avenue from Admiralty Arch to the palace gate. He will reconstruct the forecourt and the central balcony, thinking all the time how suitable it must have been for a powerful ruler whose sway extended to the remote parts of the world. Even a present-day American might be tempted to shake his head over the arrogance of a George III, enthroned in such impressive state as this. But again we find that the really powerful monarchs all lived somewhere else, in buildings long since vanished — at Greenwich or Nonesuch, Kenilworth or Whitehall. The builder of Buckingham Palace was George IV, whose court architect, John Nash, was responsible for what was described at the time as its "general feebleness and triviality of taste." But George IV himself, who lived at Carlton House or Brighton, never saw the finished work; nor did William IV, who ordered its completion. It was Queen Victoria who first took up residence there in 1837, being married from the new palace in 1840. But her first enthusiasm for Buckingham Palace was relatively short-lived. Her husband infinitely preferred Windsor and her own later preference was for Balmoral or Osborne. The splendors of Buckingham Palace are therefore to be associated, if we are to be accurate, with a later and strictly constitutional monarchy. It dates from a period when power was vested in Parliament.

It is natural, therefore, to ask at this point whether the Palace of Westminster, where the House of Commons meets, is itself a true expression of parliamentary rule. It represents beyond question a magnificent piece of planning, aptly designed for debate and yet provided with ample space for everything else — for committee meetings, for quiet study, for refreshment, and (on its terrace) for tea. It has everything a legislator could possibly desire, all incorporated in a building of immense dignity and comfort. It should date — but this we now hardly dare assume — from a period when parliamentary rule was at its height. But once again the dates refuse to fit into this pattern. The original House, where Pitt and Fox were matched in oratory, was accidentally destroyed by fire in 1834. It would appear to have been as famed for its inconvenience as for its lofty standard of debate. The present structure was begun in 1840, partly occupied in 1852, but incomplete when its architect died in 1860. It finally assumed its present appearance in about 1868. Now, by what we can no longer regard as coincidence, the decline of Parliament can be traced, without much dispute, to the Reform Act of 1867. It was in the following year that all initiative in legislation passed from Parliament to be vested in the Cabinet. The prestige attached to the letters "M.P." began sharply to decline and thenceforward the most that could be said is that "a role, though a humble one, was left for private members." The great days were over.

The same could not be said of the various Ministries, which were to gain importance in proportion to Parliament's decline. Investigation may yet serve to reveal that the India Office reached its peak of efficiency when accommodated in the Westminster Palace Hotel. What is more significant, however, is the recent development of the Colonial Office. For while the British Empire was mostly acquired at a period when the Colonial Office (in so far as there was one) occupied haphazard premises in Downing Street, a new phase of colonial policy began when the department moved into buildings actually designed for the purpose. This was in 1875 and the structure was well designed as a background for the disasters of the Boer War. But the Colonial Office gained a new lease of life during World War II. With its move to temporary and highly inconvenient premises in Great Smith Street — premises leased from the Church of England and intended for an entirely different purpose — British colonial policy entered that phase of enlightened activity which will end no doubt with the completion of the new building planned on the site of the old Westminster Hospital. It is reassuring to know that work on this site has not even begun.

But no other British example can now match in significance the story of New Delhi. Nowhere else have British architects been given the task of planning so great a capital city as the seat of government for so vast a population. The intention to found New Delhi was announced at the Imperial Durbar of 1911, King George V being at that time the Mogul's successor on what had been the Peacock Throne. Sir Edwin Lutyens then proceeded to draw up plans for a British Versailles, splendid in conception, comprehensive in detail, masterly in design, and overpowering in scale. But the stages of its progress toward completion correspond with so many steps in political collapse. The Government of India Act of 1909 had been the prelude to all that followed — the attempt on the Viceroy's life in 1912, the Declaration of 1917, the Montagu-Chelmsford Report of 1918 and its implementation in 1920. Lord Irwin actually moved into his new palace in 1929, the year in which the Indian Congress demanded independence, the year in which the Round Table Conference opened, the year before the Civil Disobedience campaign began. It would be possible, though tedious, to trace the whole story down to the day when the British finally withdrew, showing how each phase of the retreat was exactly paralleled with the completion of another triumph in civic design. What was finally achieved was no more and no less than a mausoleum.

The decline of British imperialism actually began with the general election of 1906 and the victory on that occasion of liberal and semi-socialist ideas. It need surprise no one, therefore, to observe that 1906 is the date of completion carved in imperishable granite over the British War Office doors. The campaign of Waterloo might have been directed from poky offices around the Horse Guards Parade. It was, by contrast, in surroundings of dignity that were approved the plans for attacking the Dardanelles.

The elaborate layout of the Pentagon at Arlington, Virginia, provides another significant lesson for planners. It was not completed until the later stages of World War II and, of course, the architecture of the great victory was not constructed here, but in the crowded and untidy Munitions Building on Constitution Avenue.

Even today, as the least observant visitor to Washington can see, the most monumental edifices are found to house such derelict organizations as the Departments of Commerce and Labor, while the more active agencies occupy half-completed quarters. Indeed, much of the more urgent business of government goes forward in "temporary" structures erected during World War I, and shrewdly preserved for their stimulating effect on administration. Hard by the Capitol, the visitor will also observe the imposing marble-

and-glass headquarters of the Teamsters' Union, completed not a moment too soon before the heavy hand of Congressional investigation descended on its occupants.

It is by no means certain that an influential reader of this chapter could prolong the life of a dying institution merely by depriving it of its streamlined headquarters. What he can do, however, with more confidence, is to prevent any organization strangling itself at birth. Examples abound of new institutions coming into existence with a full establishment of deputy directors, consultants and executives; all these coming together in a building specially designed for their purpose. And experience proves that such an institution will die. It is choked by its own perfection. It cannot take root for lack of soil. It cannot grow naturally for it is already grown. Fruitless by its very nature, it cannot even flower. When we see an example of such planning — when we are confronted for example by the building designed for the United Nations — the experts among us shake their heads sadly, draw a sheet over the corpse, and tiptoe quietly into the open air.

7

PERSONALITY SCREEN
OR THE COCKTAIL FORMULA

ESSENTIAL TO the technique of modern life is the Cocktail Party. Upon this institution hinges the international, the learned, and the industrial congress. Without at least one cocktail party these gatherings are known to be impossible. So far there has been too little scientific study of their function and possible use. The time has come to give this subject some careful thought. In planning a cocktail party what, exactly, do we hope to achieve?

This question can be answered in various ways, and it soon becomes evident that the same party can serve a variety of purposes. Let us take one possible object at random and see how it could be attained more completely and quickly by the application of scientific method. Take, for example, the problem of discovering the relative importance of the people there. We may assume that their official status and seniority is already known. But what of their actual importance in relation to the work being done? It often happens that the key men and women are not those of highest official standing. That these others are influential will be apparent by the end of the conference. How much more useful if we could have assessed their importance at the beginning! It is in this assessment that a cocktail party, held on the second day of the congress, may give invaluable aid.

For the purposes of the investigation it will be assumed that the space in which the party is to be held is all on one level and that there is only one formal entrance. It will be assumed, further, that the whole affair is to last two hours according to the invitation cards but two hours and twenty minutes in actual fact. It will be assumed, finally, that the drinks circulate freely throughout the area with which we have to deal; for a bar in visible operation would alter the nature of the problem. Given these assumptions, how are we to assess the real as opposed to the theoretical importance of the guests present?

The first known fact upon which we can base our theory is the direction of the human current. We know that the guests on arrival will drift automatically toward the left side of the reception floor. This leftward set of the tide has an interesting and partly biological explanation. The heart is (or to be exact, appears to be) on the left side of the body. In the more primitive form of warfare some form of shield is therefore used to protect the left side, leaving the offensive weapon to be held in the right hand. The normal offensive weapon was the sword, worn in a scabbard or sheath. If the sword was to be wielded in the right hand, the scabbard would have to be worn on the left side. With a scabbard worn on the left, it became physically impossible to mount a horse on the off side unless intending to face the tail — which was not the normal practice. But if you mount on the near side, you will want to have your horse on the left of the road, so that you are clear of the traffic while mounting. It therefore becomes natural and proper to keep to the left, the contrary practice (as adopted in some backward countries) being totally opposed to all the deepest historical instincts. Free of arbitrary traffic rules the normal human being swings to the left.

The second known fact is that people prefer the side of the room to the middle. This is obvious from the way a restaurant fills up. The tables along the left wall are occupied first, then those at the far end, then those along the right wall, and finally (and with reluctance) those in the middle. Such is the human revulsion to the central space that managements often despair of filling it and so create what is termed a dance floor. It will be realized that this behavior pattern could be upset by some extraneous factor, like a view of the waterfall from the end windows. If we exclude cathedrals and glaciers, the restaurant will fill up on the lines indicated, from left to right. Reluctance to occupy the central space derives from prehistoric instincts. The caveman who entered someone else's cave was doubtful of his reception and wanted to be able to have his back to the wall and yet with some room to maneuver. In the center of the cave he felt too vulnerable. He therefore sidled round the walls of the cave, grunting and fingering his club. Modern man is seen to do much the same thing, muttering to himself and fingering his club tie. The basic trend of movement at a cocktail party is the same as in a restaurant. The tendency is *toward* the sides of the space, but not actually reaching the wall.

If we combine these two known facts, the leftward drift and the tendency to avoid the center, we have the biological explanation of the phenomenon we have all observed

in practice: that is the clockwise flow of the human movement. There may be local eddies and swirls — women will
swerve to avoid people they detest, or rush crying "Dar-
ling!" toward people they detest even more — but the general set of the tide runs inexorably round the room. People
who matter, people who are literally "in the swim," keep
to the channel where the tide runs strongly. They move
with the general movement and at very much the average
speed. Those who appear to be glued to the walls, usually
deep in conversation with people they meet every week,
are nobodies. Those who jam themselves in the corners of
the room are the timid and feeble. Those who drift into
the center are the eccentric and merely silly.

What we have next to study is the time at which people
arrive. Now we can safely assume that the people who matter will arrive at the time they consider favorable. They will
not be among those who have overestimated the length of
their journey and so arrive ten minutes before the party is
due to begin. They will not be among those whose watches
have stopped and who rush in, panting, when the party is
nearly over. No, the people we want to identify will choose
their moment. What moment will it be? It will clearly
be a time fixed by two major considerations. They will not
want to make an entrance before there are sufficient people
there to observe their arrival. But neither will they want
to arrive after other important people have gone on (as they
always do) to another party. Their arrival will therefore be
at least half an hour after the party begins and at least an
hour before it is due to end. That gives us a bracket, sug-
gesting the formula that the optimum arrival time will be
exactly three-quarters of an hour after the time given on

73

the invitation card: 7.15, for example, if the party is supposed to start at 6.30. The temptation at this point is to conclude that the discovery of the optimum arrival time is the solution to the whole problem. Some students might say, "Never mind what happens afterwards. Observe the door with a stop watch and you have the answer." The more experienced investigator will treat that suggestion with gentle derision. For who is to know that the person arriving at 7.15 precisely was aiming to do just that? Some may arrive at that time because they meant to be there at 6.30 but could not find the place. Others may arrive at that hour thinking that the time is later than it is. A few might turn up then without even being invited — guests expected somewhere else and on another day. So, although safely concluding that the people who matter should arrive between 7.10 and 7.20, we would be entirely wrong to regard as important all who appear at about that time.

It is at this stage in the research project that we need to test and complete our theory by experimental means. Fully to understand the social current, we should resort to the technique used in a hydraulic laboratory. In such an establishment the scientist who wants to ascertain how water will flow round a bridge pier of a certain shape will add cochineal to the water which he sets flowing over a sheet of glass. On the glass he places his model pier. Then from above he photographs the pattern made by the color streaks in the water. What we should like to do would be to mark the people of *known* importance at a cocktail party — stain them, as it were, with cochineal — and photograph their progress from a gallery. It may be supposed that there are difficulties about pursuing an investigation on these lines.

Luckily, however, information came to hand about a certain British Colony where the "staining" of some specimens had already been done.

What had happened was that a former Governor, perhaps a century ago, tried to persuade the respectable male population to wear black evening dress instead of white. His persuasion and example failed completely so far as the merchants, bankers and lawyers were concerned but he was necessarily obeyed by the civil servants, who had no option in the matter. The result was that a tradition grew up and has been observed to this day. High government officers wear black and everyone else wears white. Now, as the officials are still important in this particular society, it was easy for investigators to follow their movement from a gallery. It was possible, moreover, to photograph their movement pattern on different occasions, confirming the theories so far described and leading us to the final discovery which we are now in a position to disclose. Careful observations proved, beyond a shadow of doubt, that the black coats arrived at some time between 7.10 and 7.20; that they circled left and so proceeded around the floor; that they avoided the corners and the walls; and that they shunned the middle. So far their behavior closely conformed to our theory. But we now noted a further and unexpected phenomenon. Having reached a point near the far right corner of the room — which they did in half an hour — they lingered in the same area for ten minutes or more. They then tended to leave rather abruptly. It was only after long and careful study of the films taken that we realized what this behavior meant. The pause, we finally concluded, was to allow the other important people to catch up, those who had arrived at 7.10 waiting for those who had arrived at 7.20. The actual foregathering of the important people did not take long. They each merely wanted to be seen by the others, as proof that they were there. This done, the withdrawal began and was, in every instance, complete by 8.15.

What we learned by observation in this one society is now believed to be applicable to any other; and the formula is easy to apply. To find the people who really matter, divide the whole floor area (mentally) into squares. Letter these from left to right, as you enter, as A, B, C, D, E, and F. Number the squares from the entrance to the far end as 1 to 8. The hour at which the party begins should be termed H. The moment when the last guest leaves will be approximately two hours and twenty minutes after the first people arrive. We shall call this $H + 140$. To find the people who really matter is now perfectly simple. They are the people grouped in square $E/7$ between $H + 75$ and $H + 90$. The most important person of all will be in the very center of the group.

Students will realize that the validity of this rule must depend upon its not being generally known. The contents of this chapter should therefore be treated as confidential and kept strictly under lock and key. Students of social science must keep this information to themselves and members of the general public are not on any account to read it.

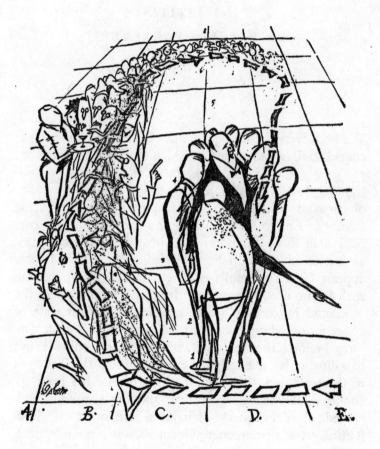

8

INJELITITIS

OR PALSIED PARALYSIS

WE FIND everywhere a type of organization (administrative, commercial, or academic) in which the higher officials are plodding and dull, those less senior are active only in intrigue against each other, and the junior men are frustrated or frivolous. Little is being attempted. Nothing is being achieved. And in contemplating this sorry picture, we conclude that those in control have done their best, struggled against adversity, and have finally admitted defeat. It now appears from the results of recent investigation, that no such failure need be assumed. In a high percentage of the moribund institutions so far examined the final state of coma is something gained of set purpose and after prolonged effort. It is the result, admittedly, of a disease, but of a disease that is largely self-induced. From the first signs of the condition, the progress of the disease has been encouraged, the causes aggravated, and the symptoms welcomed. It is the disease of induced inferiority, called Injelititis. It is a commoner ailment than is often supposed, and the diagnosis is far easier than the cure.

Our study of this organizational paralysis begins, logically, with a description of the course of the disease from the first signs to the final coma. The second stage of our in-quiry concerns symptoms and diagnosis. The third stage should properly include some reference to treatment, but little is known about this. Nor is much likely to be discovered in the immediate future, for the tradition of British medical research is entirely opposed to any emphasis on this part of the subject. British medical specialists are usually quite content to trace the symptoms and define the cause. It is the French, by contrast, who begin by describing the treatment and discuss the diagnosis later, if at all. We feel bound to adhere in this to the British method, which may not help the patient but which is unquestionably more scientific. To travel hopefully is better than to arrive.

The first sign of danger is represented by the appearance in the organization's hierarchy of an individual who combines in himself a high concentration of incompetence and jealousy. Neither quality is significant in itself and most people have a certain proportion of each. But when these two qualities reach a certain concentration — represented at present by the formula I^3J^5 — there is a chemical reaction. The two elements fuse, producing a new substance that we have termed "injelitance." The presence of this substance can be safely inferred from the actions of any individual who, having failed to make anything of his own department, tries constantly to interfere with other departments and gain control of the central administration. The specialist who observes this particular mixture of failure and ambition will at once shake his head and murmur, "Primary or idiopathic injelitance." The symptoms, as we shall see, are quite unmistakable.

The next or secondary stage in the progress of the disease is reached when the infected individual gains complete or partial control of the central organization. In many instances this stage is reached without any period of primary infection, the individual having actually entered the organization at that level. The injelitant individual is easily recognizable at this stage from the persistence with which he struggles to eject all those abler than himself, as also from his resistance to the appointment or promotion of

anyone who might prove abler in course of time. He dare not say, "Mr. Asterisk is too able," so he says, "Asterisk? Clever perhaps — but is he *sound?* I incline to prefer Mr. Cypher." He dare not say, "Mr. Asterisk makes me feel small," so he says, "Mr. Cypher appears to me to have the better judgment." Judgment is an interesting word that signifies in this context the opposite of intelligence; it means, in fact, doing what was done last time. So Mr. Cypher is promoted and Mr. Asterisk goes elsewhere. The central administration gradually fills up with people stupider than the chairman, director, or manager. If the head of the organization is second-rate, he will see to it that his immediate staff are all third-rate; and they will, in turn, see to it that their subordinates are fourth-rate. There will soon be an actual competition in stupidity, people pretending to be even more brainless than they are.

The next or tertiary stage in the onset of this disease is reached when there is no spark of intelligence left in the whole organization from top to bottom. This is the state of coma we described in our first paragraph. When that stage has been reached the institution is, for all practical purposes, dead. It may remain in a coma for twenty years. It may quietly disintegrate. It may even, finally, recover. Cases of recovery are rare. It may be thought odd that recovery without treatment should be possible. The process is quite natural, nevertheless, and closely resembles the process by which various living organisms develop a resistance to poisons that are at first encounter fatal. It is as if the whole institution had been sprayed with a DDT solution guaranteed to eliminate all ability found in its way. For a period of years this practice achieves the desired result. Eventually, however, individuals develop an immunity. They conceal their ability under a mask of imbecile good humor. The result is that the operatives assigned to the task of ability-elimination fail (through stupidity) to recognize ability when they see it. An individual of merit penetrates the outer defenses and begins to make his way toward the top. He wanders on, babbling about golf and giggling feebly, losing documents and forgetting names, and looking just like everyone else. Only when he has reached high rank does he suddenly throw off the mask and appear like the demon king among a crowd of pantomime fairies. With shrill screams of dismay the high executives find ability right there in the midst of them. It is too late by then to do anything about it. The damage has been done, the disease is in retreat, and full recovery is possible over the next ten years. But these instances of natural cure are extremely rare. In the more usual course of events, the disease passes through the recognized stages and becomes, as it would seem, incurable.

We have seen what the disease is. It now remains to show by what symptoms its presence can be detected. It is one thing to detail the spread of the infection in an imaginary case, classified from the start. It is quite a different thing to enter a factory, barracks, office, or college and recognize the symptoms at a glance. We all know how an estate agent will wander round a vacant house when acting for the purchaser. It is only a question of time before he throws open a cupboard or kicks a baseboard and exclaims, "Dry rot!" (acting for the vendor, he would lose the key of the cupboard while drawing attention to the view from the window). In the same way a political scientist can recognize the symptoms of Injelititis even in its primary stage. He will pause, sniff, and nod wisely, and it should be obvious at once that he knows. But how does he know? How can he tell that injelitance has set in? If the original source of the infection were present, the diagnosis would be easier, but it is still quite possible when the germ of the disease is on holiday. His influence can be detected in the atmosphere. It can be detected, above all, in certain remarks that will be made by others, as thus: "It would be a mistake for us to attempt too much. We cannot compete with Toprank. Here in Lowgrade we do useful work, meeting the needs of the country. Let us be content with that." Or again, "We do not pretend to be in the first flight. It is absurd the way these people at Much-Striving talk of their work, just as if they were in the Toprank class." Or finally, "Some of our younger men have transferred to Toprank — one or two even to Much-Striving. It is probably their wisest plan. We are quite happy to let them succeed in that way. An exchange of ideas and personnel is a good thing — although, to be sure, the few men we have had from Toprank have been rather disappointing. We can only expect the people they have thrown out. Ah well, we must not grumble. We always avoid friction when we can. And, in our humble way we can claim to be doing a good job."

What do these remarks suggest? They suggest — or, rather, they clearly indicate — that the standard of achievement has been set too low. Only a low standard is desired and one still lower is acceptable. The directives issuing from a second-rate chief and addressed to his third-rate executives speak only of minimum aims and ineffectual means. A higher standard of competence is not desired, for an efficient organization would be beyond the chief's power to control. The motto, "Ever third-rate" has been inscribed over the main entrance in letters of gold. Third-rateness has become a principle of policy. It will be observed, however, that the existence of higher standards is still recognized. There remains at this primary stage a hint of apology, a feeling of uneasiness when Toprank is mentioned. Neither this apology nor unease lasts for long. The second stage of the disease comes on quickly and it is this we must now describe.

The secondary stage is recognized by its chief symptom, which is Smugness. The aims have been set low and have therefore been largely achieved. The target has been set up within ten yards of the firing point and the scoring has therefore been high. The directors have done what they set out to do. This soon fills them with self-satisfaction. They set out to do something and they have done it. They soon forget that it was a small effort to gain a small result. They observe only that they have succeeded — unlike those people at Much-Striving. They become increasingly smug and their smugness reveals itself in remarks such as this: "The chief is a sound man and very clever when you get to know him. He never says much — that is not his way — but he seldom makes a mistake." (These last words can be said with justice of someone who never does anything at all.) Or this: "We rather distrust brilliance here. These clever people can be a dreadful nuisance, upsetting established routine and proposing all sorts of schemes that we have never seen tried. We obtain splendid results by simple common sense and teamwork." And finally this: "Our canteen is something we are really rather proud of. We don't know how the caterer can produce so good a lunch at the price. We are lucky to have him!" This last remark is made as we sit at a table covered with dirty oilcloth, facing an uneatable, nameless mess on a plate and shuddering at the sight and smell of what passes for coffee. In point of fact, the canteen reveals more than the office. Just as for a quick verdict we judge a private house by inspection of the WC (to find whether there is a spare toilet roll), just as we judge a hotel by the state of the cruet, so we judge a larger institution by the appearance of the canteen. If the decoration is in dark brown and pale green; if the curtains are purple(or absent); if there are no flowers in sight; if there is barley in the soup (with or without a dead fly); if the menu is one of hash and mold; and if the executives are still delighted with everything — why, then the institution is in a pretty bad way. For self-satisfaction, in such a case, has reached the point at which those responsible cannot tell the difference between food and filth. This is smugness made absolute.

The tertiary and last stage of the disease is one in which apathy has taken the place of smugness. The executives no longer boast of their efficiency as compared with some other institution. They have forgotten that any other institution exists. They have ceased to eat in the canteen, preferring now to bring sandwiches and scatter their desks with the crumbs. The bulletin boards carry notices about the concert that took place four years ago, Mr. Brown's office has a nameplate saying, "Mr. Smith." Mr. Smith's door is marked, "Mr. Robinson," in faded ink on an adhesive luggage label. The broken windows have been repaired with odd bits of cardboard. The electric light switches give a slight but painful shock when touched. The whitewash is flaking off the ceiling and the paint is blotchy on the walls. The elevator is out of order and the cloakroom tap cannot be turned off. Water from the broken skylight drips wide of the bucket placed to catch it, and from somewhere in the basement comes the wail of a hungry cat. The last stage of the disease has brought the whole organization to the point of collapse. The symptoms of the disease in this acute form are so numerous and evident that a trained investigator can often detect them over the telephone without visiting the place at all. When a weary voice answers "Ullo!" (that most unhelpful of replies), the expert has often heard enough. He shakes his head sadly as he replaces the receiver. "Well on in the tertiary phase," he will mutter to himself, "and almost certainly inoperable." It is too late to attempt any sort of treatment. The institution is practically dead.

We have now described this disease as seen from within and then again from outside. We know now the origin, the progress, and the outcome of the infection, as also the symptoms by which its presence is detected. British medical skill seldom goes beyond that point in its research. Once a disease has been identified, named, described, and accounted for, the British are usually quite satisfied and ready to investigate the next problem that presents itself. If asked about treatment they look surprised and suggest the use of penicillin preceded or followed by the extraction of all the patient's teeth. It becomes clear at once that this is not an aspect of the subject that interests them. Should our attitude be the same? Or should we as political scientists consider what, if anything, can be done about it? It would be premature, no doubt, to discuss any possible treatment in detail, but it might be useful to indicate very generally the lines along which a solution might be attempted. Certain principles, at least, might be laid down. Of such principles, the first would have to be this: a diseased institution cannot reform itself. There are instances, we know, of a disease vanishing without treatment, just as it appeared without warning; but these cases are rare and regarded by the specialist as irregular and undesirable. The cure, whatever its nature, must come from outside. For a patient to remove his own appendix under a local anaesthetic may be physically possible, but the practice is regarded with disfavor and is open to many objections. Other operations lend themselves still less to the patient's own dexterity. The first principle we can safely enunciate is that the patient and the surgeon should not be the same person. When an institution is in an advanced state of disease, the services of a specialist are required and even, in some instances, the services of the greatest living authority: Parkinson himself. The fees payable may be very heavy indeed, but in a case of this sort, expense is clearly no object. It is a matter, after all, of life and death.

The second principle we might lay down is this, that the primary stage of the disease can be treated by a simple injection, that the secondary stage can be cured in some instances by surgery, and that the tertiary stage must be regarded at present as incurable. There was a time when physicians used to babble about bottles and pills, but this is mainly out of date. There was another period when they talked more vaguely about psychology; but that too is out of date, most of the psychoanalysts having since been certi-

fied as insane. The present age is one of injections and in-
cisions and it behooves the political scientists to keep in
step with the Faculty. Confronted by a case of primary infection, we prepare a syringe automatically and only hesi-
tate as to what, besides water, it should contain. In principle, the injection should contain some active substance
— but from which group should it be selected? A kill-
or-cure injection would contain a high proportion of Intolerance, but this drug is difficult to procure and sometimes too powerful to use. Intolerance is obtainable from
the bloodstream of regimental sergeant majors and is found
to comprise two chemical elements, namely: (a) the best
is scarcely good enough (GG^{nth}) and (b) there is no excuse for anything (NE^{nth}). Injected into a diseased institution, the intolerant individual has a tonic effect and may
cause the organism to turn against the original source of
infection. While this treatment may well do good, it is by
no means certain that the cure will be permanent. It is
doubtful, that is to say, whether the infected substance will
be actually expelled from the system. Such information as
we have rather leads us to suppose that this treatment is
merely palliative in the first instance, the disease remaining
latent though inactive. Some authorities believe that repeated injections would result in a complete cure, but
others fear that repetition of the treatment would set up
a fresh irritation, only slightly less dangerous than the original disease. Intolerance is a drug to be used, therefore,
with caution.

There exists a rather milder drug called Ridicule, but its
operation is uncertain, its character unstable, and its effects
too little known. There is little reason to fear that any

damage could result from an injection of ridicule, but neither is it evident that a cure would result. It is generally agreed that the injelitant individual will have developed a thick protective skin, insensitive to ridicule. It may well be that ridicule may tend to isolate the infection, but that is as much as could be expected and more indeed than has been claimed.

We may note, finally, that Castigation, which is easily obtainable, has been tried in cases of this sort and not wholly without effect. Here again, however, there are difficulties. This drug is an immediate stimulus but can produce a result the exact opposite of what the specialist intends. After a momentary spasm of activity, the injelitant individual will often prove more supine than before and just as harmful as a source of infection. If any use can be made of castigation it will almost certainly be as one element in a preparation composed otherwise of intolerance and ridicule, with perhaps other drugs as yet untried. It only remains to point out that this preparation does not as yet exist.

The secondary stage of the disease we believe to be operable. Professional readers will all have heard of the Nuciform Sack and of the work generally associated with the name of Cutler Walpole. The operation first performed by that great surgeon involves, simply, the removal of the infected parts and the simultaneous introduction of new blood drawn from a similar organism. This operation has sometimes succeeded. It is only fair to add that it has also sometimes failed. The shock to the system can be too great. The new blood may be unobtainable and may fail, even when procured, to mingle with the blood previously in circulation. On the other hand, this drastic method offers, beyond question, the best chance of a complete cure.

The tertiary stage presents us with no opportunity to do anything. The institution is for all practical purposes dead. It can be founded afresh but only with a change of name, a change of site, and an entirely different staff. The temptation, for the economically minded, is to transfer some portion of the original staff to the new institution — in the name, for example, of continuity. Such a transfusion would certainly be fatal, and continuity is the very thing to avoid. No portion of the old and diseased foundation can be regarded as free from infection. No staff, no equipment, no tradition must be removed from the original site. Strict quarantine should be followed by complete disinfection. Infected personnel should be dispatched with a warm testimonial to such rival institutions as are regarded with particular hostility. All equipment and files should be destroyed without hesitation. As for the buildings, the best plan is to insure them heavily and then set them alight. Only when the site is a blackened ruin can we feel certain that the germs of the disease are dead.

9

PALM THATCH TO PACKARD
OR A FORMULA FOR, SUCCESS

READERS WHO are all too familiar with popular works on anthropology may be interested to learn that some recent investigations have involved a completely novel approach. The ordinary anthropologist is one who spends six weeks or six months (or even sometimes six years) among, say, the Boreyu tribe at their settlement on the Upper Teedyas River, Darndreeryland. He then returns to civilization with his photographs, tape recorders, and notebooks, eager to write his book about sex life and superstition. For tribes such as the Boreyu, life is made intolerable by all this peering and prying. They often become converts to Presbyterianism in the belief that they will thereupon cease to be of interest to anthropologists; nor in fact has this device been known to fail. But enough primitive people remain for the purposes of science. Books continue to multiply, and when the last tribe has resorted to the singing of hymns in self-defense, there are still the poor of the backstreets. These are perpetually pursued by questionnaire, camera, and phonograph; and the written results are familiar to us all. What is new about the approach now being attempted is not the technique of investigation but the choice of a so-

ciety in which to work. Anthropologists of this latest school
ignore the primitive and have no time for the poor. They
prefer to do their fieldwork among the rich.

The team whose work we shall now describe, and to which
the present author is attached, made certain preliminary
studies among Greek Shipping Magnates and went on to
deal in greater detail with the Arab Chieftains of the Pipe-
line. When this line of investigation had to be abandoned,
for political and other reasons, the team went on to study
the Chinese Millionaires of Singapore. It is there we encountered the Flunky Puzzle. It is there we first heard of
the Chinese Hound Barrier. During the early stages of our
inquiry we did not know the meaning of either term. We
did not even know whether they were different names for
the same thing. What we can claim now is that we at least
followed up the first clue to present itself.

This clue we obtained in the course of a visit to the
Singapore palace of Mr. Hu Got Dow. Turning to the
equerry who had shown him round the millionaire's col-
lection of jade, Dr. Meddleton exclaimed, "Gee, and they
say he began life as a coolie!" To this the inscrutable
Chinese replied, "Only coolie can become millionaire.
Only coolie can look like coolie. Only velly lich man can
afford to look lich." Upon these few and enigmatic words
(of which no further explanation was offered) we based
our whole scheme of research. The detailed results are comprised in the Meddleton-Snooperage Report (1956) but
there is no reason why they should not be presented in a
simplified form for the general reader. What follows is
just such an outline, with technicalities mostly omitted.

Up to a point, as we recognized, the problem of the

coolie-millionaire offers no real difficulty. The Chinese coolie lives in a palm-thatched hovel on a bowl of rice. When he has risen to a higher occupation — hawking peanuts, for example, from a barrow — he still lives on rice and still lives in a hovel. When he has risen farther — to the selling, say, of possibly stolen bicycle parts, he keeps to his hovel and his rice. The result is that he has money to invest. Of ten coolies in this situation, nine will lose their money by unwise speculation. The tenth will be clever or lucky. He will live, nevertheless, in his hovel. He will eat, as before, his rice. As a success technique this is well worthy of study.

In the American log cabin story the point is soon reached at which the future millionaire must wear a tie. He explains that he cannot otherwise inspire confidence. He must also acquire a better address, purely (he says) to gain prestige. In point of fact, the tie is to please his wife and the address to satisfy his daughter. The Chinese have their womenfolk under better control. So the prosperous coolie sticks to his hovel and his rice. This is a known fact and admits of two explanations. In the first place his home (whatever its other disadvantages) has undeniably brought him luck. In the second place, a better house would unquestionably attract the notice of the tax collector. So he wisely stays where he is. He will often keep the original hovel — at any rate as an office — for the rest of his life. He quits it so reluctantly that his decision to move marks a major crisis in his career.

When he moves it is primarily to evade the exactions of secret societies, blackmailers, and gangs. To conceal his growing wealth from the tax collector is a relatively easy matter; but to conceal it from his business associates is practically impossible. Once the word goes round that he is prospering, accurate guesses will be made as to the sum for which he can be "touched." All this is admittedly well known, but previous investigators have jumped too readily to the conclusion that there is only one sum involved. In point of fact there are three: the sum the victim would pay if kidnaped and held to ransom; the sum he would pay to keep a defamatory article out of a Chinese newspaper; the sum he would subscribe to charity rather than lose face.

Our task was to ascertain the figure the first sum will have reached (on an average) at the moment when migration takes place from the original hovel to a well-fenced house guarded by an Alsatian hound. It is this move that has been termed "Breaking the Hound Barrier." Social scientists believe that it will tend to occur as soon as the ransom to be exacted comes to exceed the overhead costs of the "snatch."

At about the time a prosperous Chinese changes house he has also to acquire a Chevrolet or Packard. Such a purchase often, however, antedates the change of address. So the spectacle of the expensive car outside the dingy office is too familiar to arouse much comment. No complete explanation has so far been offered. Conceding, as we may, the need for a car, we should rather expect it to share the squalor of its surroundings. For reasons not yet apparent, however, Chinese prosperity is first and fairly measured in terms of chromium, upholstery, make, and year. And the Packard will involve, very soon, a wire fence, barred windows, padlocked garage, and hound. A revolutionary change has occurred. If the Alsatian-owner does not go so far as to pay his taxes, he must at least know how to explain why no taxable income has so far come his way. And supposing he can avoid paying $100,000 to gangsters, he can hardly avoid payment of blackmail in some form. He must expect to receive obsequious journalists who claim credit for refusing to publish hostile articles about him in dubious journals. He must expect to see the same journalists a week later, this time collecting funds for some vaguely described orphanage. He must accustom himself to the visits of trade union officials offering for a consideration to discourage the industrial unrest that will otherwise affect his interests. He must resign himself, in fact, to the loss of a percentage.

One of our objects was to compile some detailed information about the Alsatian-owning phase of a Chinese businessman's career. This was, in some ways, the most difficult part of the whole investigation. There are types of knowledge only to be gained at the price of torn trousers and bandaged ankles. We are proud to think, in retrospect, that where risks were inevitable they were taken unflinchingly. No fieldwork was needed, however, to discover what actual amounts are paid in ransom. These figures are in fact generally known and often quoted in the local press with some pretense at accuracy. What is significant about these figures is the range between the smallest and the largest figures quoted. Sums appear to vary from $5000 to $200,000 — never as little as $2000 nor as much as $500,-000. Nor can there be any doubt that the majority of extortions fall within a narrower range than that. Further research will, no doubt, establish what the average amount can be taken to be.

If we suppose that the minimum extortion represents a figure just high enough to yield a marginal profit, we shall as readily conclude that the maximum extortion represents all that can be extracted from the richest men that are ever kidnaped. It is manifest, however, that the very wealthiest men are never kidnaped at all. There would seem to be a point beyond which the Chinese gains immunity from blackmail. In this last phase, moreover, the millionaire

seeks to emphasize rather than conceal his wealth, demonstrating publicly that the point of immunity has been reached. So far, no social scientist of our team has been able to discover how this final immunity is achieved. Several have been thrown out of the Millionaires' Club when trying to collect evidence on this point. Concluding that it has something to do with the number of equerries, aides-de-camp, personal assistants, secretaries, and valets (all much in evidence at this stage) they have termed the problem "The Flunky Puzzle" and left it at that.

It is not to be supposed however that this problem will baffle us for long. Indeed, we know already that our choice lies, broadly speaking, between two alternative explanations, with the proviso that we may possibly end by accepting both. One guess has been that the flunkies are really gunmen forming an impenetrable bodyguard. The other guess is that the millionaire has bought up an entire secret society and one against which no other gang dare act. To test the former theory — by a carefully staged holdup — would be relatively simple. At the cost of a life or two the fact could be established beyond all reasonable doubt. To test the latter theory would need more brains and possibly more courage. With several casualties already among the brave dog-bitten members of our team, we did not feel justified in pursuing this line of research. We concluded that we had neither the men nor the funds to complete the investigation. Having since received timely aid from the Miss Plaste Trust (Far East branch) we hope to know the answer fairly soon.

A problem that remains, even after the publication of our interim report, is the enigma of Chinese tax evasion.

All that we could discover about this was that Western methods are not widely used. As is well known, the Western technique depends on discovering the standard delay (or S.D., as we call it among ourselves) in the department with which we have to deal. That is, of course, the normal lapse of time between the receipt of a letter and its being dealt with. It is, to be more exact, the time it takes for a file to rise from the bottom of the in-tray to the top of the pile. Supposing this to be twenty-seven days, the Western tax evader begins his campaign by writing to ask why he has received no notice of assessment. It does not matter, actually, what he says in the letter. All he wants is to ensure that his file, with its new enclosure, will be at the bottom of the heap. *Twenty-five days later* he will write again, asking why his first letter has not been answered. This sends his file back to the bottom again just when it was almost reaching the top. Twenty-five days later he writes again. . . . So his file is never dealt with at all and never in fact comes into view. This being the method known to us all, and known to be successful, we naturally concluded that it was known also to the Chinese. We found, however, that there is no S.D. in the East. Owing to variations in climate and sobriety, the government departments lack that ordered rhythm which would make them predictable. Whatever method the Chinese use, it cannot depend upon a known S.D.

To this problem we have, it should be emphasized, no final solution. All we have is a theory upon the validity of which it would be premature to comment. It was put forward by one of our most brilliant investigators and can be described as no more than an inspired guess. According to this supposition the Chinese millionaire does not wait for his assessment, but prefers to send the tax collector a check in advance for, say, $329.83. A covering note refers briefly to earlier correspondence and a previous sum paid in cash. The effect of this maneuver is to throw the whole tax-collecting machine out of gear. Disorganization turns to chaos when a further letter arrives, apologizing for the error and asking for twenty-three cents back. Officials are so perturbed and mystified that they produce no response of any kind for about eighteen months — and another check reaches them before that period has elapsed, this time for $167.42. In this way, the theory goes, the millionaire pays virtually nothing and the inspector of taxes ends in a padded cell. Unproved as this theory may be, it seems worthy of careful investigation. We might at least give it a trial.

10
PENSION POINT
OR THE AGE OF RETIREMENT

OF THE MANY problems discussed and solved in this work,
it is proper that the question of retirement should be left
to the last. It has been the subject of many commissions of
inquiry but the evidence heard has always been hopelessly
conflicting and the final recommendations muddled, incon-
clusive, and vague. Ages of compulsory retirement are fixed
at points varying from 55 to 75, all being equally arbitrary
and unscientific. Whatever age has been decreed by accident and custom can be defended by the same argument.
Where the retirement age is fixed at 65 the defenders of
this system will always have found, by experience, that the
mental powers and energy show signs of flagging at the age
of 62. This would be a most useful conclusion to have
reached had not a different phenomenon been observed in
organizations where the age of retirement has been fixed at
60. There, we are told, people are found to lose their grip,
in some degree, at the age of 57. As against that, men
whose retiring age is 55 are known to be past their best at
52. It would seem, in short, that efficiency declines at the
age of R minus 3, irrespective of the age at which R has
been fixed. This is an interesting fact in itself but not

directly helpful when it comes to deciding what the R age is to be.

But while the R — 3 age is not directly useful to us, it may serve to suggest that the investigations hitherto pursued have been on the wrong lines. The observation often made that men vary, some being old at 50, others still energetic at 80 or 90, may well be true, but here again the fact leads us nowhere. The truth is that the age of retirement should not be related in any way to the man whose retirement we are considering. It is his successor we have to watch: the man (Y) destined to replace the other man (X) when the latter retires. He will pass, as is well known, the following stages in his successful career:

1. Age of Qualification   =   Q
2. Age of Discretion   =   D $(Q + 3)$
3. Age of Promotion   =   P $(D + 7)$
4. Age of Responsibility =   R $(P + 5)$
5. Age of Authority   =   A $(R + 3)$
6. Age of Achievement   =   AA $(A + 7)$
7. Age of Distinction   =   DD $(AA + 9)$
8. Age of Dignity   =   DDD $(DD + 6)$
9. Age of Wisdom   =   W $(DDD + 3)$
10. Age of Obstruction   =   OO $(W + 7)$

The above scale is governed by the numerical value of Q. Now, Q is to be understood as a technical term. It does not mean that a man at Q knows anything of the business he will have to transact. Architects, for example, pass some form of examination but are seldom found to know anything useful at that point (or indeed any other point) in their career. The term Q means the age at which a professional or business career begins, usually after an elaborate training that has proved profitable only to those paid for organizing it. It will be seen that if $Q = 22$, X will not reach OO (the Age of Obstruction) until he is 72. So far as his own efficiency is concerned, there is no valid reason for replacing him until he is 71. But our problem centers not on him but on Y, his destined successor. How are the ages of X and Y likely to compare? To be more exact, how old will X have been when Y first entered the department or firm?

This problem has been the subject of prolonged investigation. Our inquiries have tended to prove that the age gap between X and Y is exactly fifteen years. (It is not, we find, the normal practice for the son to succeed the father directly.) Taking this average of fifteen years, and assuming that $Q = 22$, we find that Y will have reached AA (the Age of Achievement) at 47, when X is only 62. And that, clearly, is where the crisis occurs. For Y, if thwarted in his ambition through X's still retaining control, enters, it has been proved, a different series of stages in his career. These stages are as follows:

6. Age of Frustration   (F) $= A + 7$
7. Age of Jealousy   (J) $= F + 9$
8. Age of Resignation (R) $= J + 4$
9. Age of Oblivion   (O) $= R + 5$

When X, therefore, is 72, Y is 57, just entering on the Age of Resignation. Should X at last retire at that age, Y is quite unfit to take his place, being now resigned (after

a decade of frustration and jealousy) to a career of medi-
ocrity. For Y, opportunity will have come just ten years
too late.

The age of Frustration will not always be the same in
years, depending as it does on the factor Q, but its symptoms are easy to recognize. The man who is denied the
opportunity of taking decisions of importance begins to

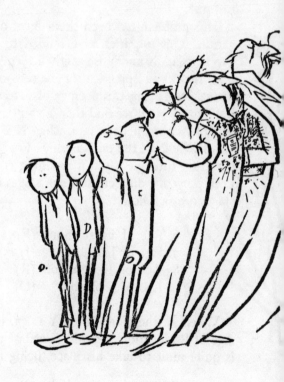

regard as important the decisions he is allowed to take. He becomes fussy about filing, keen on seeing that pencils are sharpened, eager to ensure that the windows are open (or shut), and apt to use two or three different-colored inks. The Age of Jealousy reveals itself in an emphasis upon seniority. "After all, I am still somebody." "I was never consulted." "Z has very little experience." But that period

gives place to the Age of Resignation. "I am not one of these ambitious types." "Z is welcome to a seat on the Board — more trouble than it is worth, I should say." "Promotion would only have interfered with my golf." The theory has been advanced that the Age of Frustration is also marked by an interest in local politics. It is now known, however, that men enter local politics solely as a result of being unhappily married. It will be apparent, however, from the other symptoms described, that the man still in a subordinate position at 47 (or equivalent) will never be fit for anything else.

The problem, it is now clear, is to make X retire at the age of 60, while still able to do the work better than anyone else. The immediate change may be for the worse but the alternative is to have no possible successor at hand when X finally goes. And the more outstanding X has proved to be, and the longer his period of office, the more hopeless is the task of replacing him. Those nearest him in the seniority are already too old and have been subordinate for too long. All they can do is to block the way for anyone junior to them; a task in which they will certainly not fail. No competent successor will appear for years, nor at all until some crisis has brought a new leader to the fore. So the hard decision has to be taken. Unless X goes in good time, the whole organization will eventually suffer. But how is X to be moved?

In this, as in so many other matters, modern science is not at a loss. The crude methods of the past have been superseded. In days gone by it was usual, no doubt, for the other directors to talk inaudibly at board meetings, one merely opening and shutting his mouth and another nodding in apparent comprehension, thus convincing the chairman that he was actually going deaf. But there is a modern technique that is far more effective and certain. The method depends essentially on air travel and the filling in of forms. Research has shown that complete exhaustion in modern life results from a combination of these two activities. The high official who is given enough of each will very soon begin to talk of retirement. It used to be the custom in primitive African tribes to liquidate the king or chief at a certain point in his career, either after a period of years or at the moment when his vital powers appeared to have gone. Nowadays the technique is to lay before the great man the program of a conference at Helsinki in June, a congress at Adelaide in July, and a convention at Ottawa in August, each lasting about three weeks. He is assured that the prestige of the department or firm will depend on his presence and that the delegation of this duty to anyone else would be regarded as an insult by all others taking part. The program of travel will allow of his return to the office for about three or four days between one conference and the next. He will find his in-tray piled high on each occasion with forms to fill in, some relating to his travels, some to do with applications for permits or quota allocations, and the rest headed "Income Tax." On his completion of the forms awaiting his signature after the Ottawa convention, he will be given the program for a new series of conferences; one at Manila in September, the second at Mexico City in October, and the third at Quebec in November. By December he will admit that he is feeling his age. In January he will announce his intention to retire.

The essence of this technique is so to arrange matters

that the conferences are held at places the maximum distance apart and in climates offering the sharpest contrast in heat and cold. There should be no possibility whatever of a restful sea voyage in any part of the schedule. It must be air travel all the way. No particular care need be taken in the choice between one route and another. All are alike in being planned for the convenience of the mails rather than the passengers. It can safely be assumed, almost without inquiry, that most flights will involve takeoff at 2.50 A.M., reporting at the airfield at 1.30 and weighing baggage at the terminal at 12.45. Arrival will be scheduled for 3.10 A.M. on the next day but one. The aircraft will invariably, however, be somewhat overdue, touching down in fact at 3.57 A.M., so that passengers will be clear of customs and immigration by about 4.35. Going one way around the world, it is possible and indeed customary to have breakfast about three times. In the opposite direction the passengers will have nothing to eat for hours at a stretch, being finally offered a glass of sherry when on the point of collapse from malnutrition. Most of the flight time will of course be spent in filling in various declarations about currency and health. How much have you in dollars (U.S.), pounds (sterling), francs, marks, guilders, yen, lire, and pounds (Australian); how much in letters of credit, travelers checks, postage stamps, and postal orders? Where did you sleep last night and the night before that? (This last is an easy question, for the air traveler is usually able to declare, in good faith, that he has not slept at all for the past week.) When were you born and what was your grandmother's maiden name? How many children have you and why? What will be the length of your stay and where? What is the object of your visit, if any? (As if by now you could even remember.) Have you had chicken pox and why not? Have you a visa for Patagonia and a re-entry permit for Hongkong? The penalty for making a false declaration is life imprisonment. Fasten your seat belts, please. We are about to land at Rangoon. Local time is 2.47 A.M. Outside temperature is 110° F. We shall stop here for approximately one hour. Breakfast will be served on the aircraft five hours after takeoff. Thank you. (For what, in heaven's name?) No smoking, please.

It will be observed that air travel, considered as a retirement-accelerator, has the advantage of including a fair amount of form-filling. But form-filling proper is a separate ordeal, not necessarily connected with travel. The art of devising forms to be filled in depends on three elements: obscurity, lack of space, and the heaviest penalties for failure. In a form-compiling department, obscurity is ensured by various branches dealing respectively with ambiguity, irrelevance, and jargon. But some of the simpler devices have now become automatic. Thus, a favorite opening gambit is a section, usually in the top right-hand corner, worded thus:

| Return rendered in respect of the month of | |

As you have been sent the form on February 16, you have no idea whether it relates to last month, this month or next. Only the sender knows that, but he is asking you. At this point the ambiguity expert takes over, collaborating closely with a space consultant, and this is the result:

Cross out the word which does not apply	Full name	Address	Domicile	When naturalized and why	Status
Mr. Mrs. Miss					

Such a form as this is especially designed, of course, for a Colonel, Lord, Professor, or Doctor called Alexander Winthrop Percival Blenkinsop-Fotheringay of Battleaxe Towers, Layer-de-la-Haye, near Newcastle-under-Lyme, Lincolnshire-parts-of-Kesteven (whatever that may mean). Follows the word "Domicile," which is practically meaningless except to an international lawyer, and after that a mysterious reference to naturalization. Lastly, we have the word "Status," which leaves the filler-in wondering whether to put "Admiral (Ret'd)" "Married," "American Citizen" or "Managing Director."

Now the ambiguity expert hands over the task to a specialist in irrelevance, who calls in a new space allocator to advise on layout:

Number of your identity card or passport	Your grandfather's full name	Your grandmother's maiden name	Have you been vaccinated, inoculated; when & why	Give full details
Note: The penalty for furnishing incorrect information may be a fine of £5000 or a year's penal servitude, or quite possibly both.				

Then the half-completed work of art is sent to the jargon specialist, who produces something on these lines:

> What special circumstances[253] are alleged to justify the adjusted allocation for which request is made in respect of the quota period to which the former application[143] relates, whether or not the former level had been revised and in what sense and for what purpose and whether this or any previous application made by any other party or parties has been rejected by any other planning authority under subsection VII[35] or for any other reason, and whether this or the latter decision was made the subject of an appeal and with what result and why.

Finally, the form goes to the technician, who adds the space-for-signature section, the finish that crowns the whole.

> I/we [block capitals] .... declare under penalty that all the information I/we have furnished above is true to the best of my/our knowledge, as witness my/our signature signed this .... day of .... 19 ....,
> (*Signature*) ....
>
> WITNESS:
> Name ....   Photograph   *Seal* ....
> Address ....   Passport
> Occupation ....   Size   *Thumb print*

This is quite straightforward except for the final touch of confusion as to whose photograph or thumb print is wanted, the I/we person or the witness. It probably does not matter, anyway.

Experiment has shown that an elderly man in a responsible position will soon be forced to retire if given sufficient air travel and sufficient forms. Instances are frequent, moreover, of such elderly men deciding to retire before the treatment has even begun. At the first mention of a conference at Stockholm or Vancouver, they often realize that their time has arrived. Very rarely nowadays is it necessary to adopt methods of a severe character. The last recorded resort to these was in a period soon after the conclusion of World War II. The high official concerned was particularly tough and the only remedy found was to send him on a tour of tin mines and rubber estates in Malaya. This method is best tried in January, and with jet aircraft to make the climatic transition more abrupt. On landing at 5.52 P.M. (Malayan time) this official was rushed off at once to a cocktail party, from that to another cocktail party (held at a house fifteen miles from the hotel where the first took place), and from that to a dinner party (eleven miles in the opposite direction). He was in bed by about 2.30 A.M. and on board an aircraft at seven the next morning. Landing at Ipoh in time for a belated breakfast, he was then taken to visit two rubber estates, a tin mine, an oil-palm plantation, and a factory for canning pineapples. After lunch, given by the Rotary Club, he was taken to a school, a clinic, and a community center. There followed two cocktail parties and a Chinese banquet of twenty courses, the numerous toasts being drunk in neat brandy served in tumblers. The formal discussion on policy began next morning and lasted for three days, the meetings interspersed with formal receptions and nightly banquets in Sumatran or Indian style. That the treatment was too severe was fairly apparent by the fifth day, during the afternoon of which the distinguished visitor could walk only when supported by a secretary on one side, a personal assistant on the other. On the sixth day he died, thus confirming the general impression that he must have been tired or unwell. Such methods as these are now discountenanced, and have since indeed proved needless. People are learning to retire in time.

But a serious problem remains. What are we ourselves to do when nearing the retirement age we have fixed for others? It will be obvious at once that our own case is entirely different from any other case we have so far considered. We do not claim to be outstanding in any way, but it just so happens that there is no possible successor in sight. It is with genuine reluctance that we agree to postpone our retirement for a few years, purely in the public interest. And when a senior member of staff approaches us with details of a conference at Teheran or Hobart, we promptly wave it aside, announcing that all conferences are a waste of time. "Besides," we continue blandly, "my arrangements are already made. I shall be salmon fishing for the next two months and will return to this office at the end of October, by which date I shall expect all the forms to have been filled in. Goodbye until then." We knew how to make our predecessors retire. When it comes to forcing our own retirement, our successors must find some method of their own.